In the Clear

In the Clear

A Contemporary Canadian Poetry Anthology

Editors

Allan Forrie, Patrick O'Rourke, Glen Sorestad

Thistledown Press Ltd.

Canadian Cataloguing in Publication Data

In the clear

Poems
ISBN 1-895449-84-7

1. Canadian poetry (English) — 20th century.*
I. Forrie, Allan, 1948- II. O'Rourke, Patrick, 1943- III. Sorestad, Glen A., 1937-

PS8293.I53 1998   C811'.5408   C98-920060-4

Book and cover design by J. Forrie
Typeset by Thistledown Press Ltd.
Cover painting *Zing, Zip and Zap* by Jude Clarke

Printed and bound in Canada by
Veilleux Impression à Demande
Boucherville, Quebec

Thistledown Press Ltd.
633 Main Street
Saskatoon, Saskatchewan
S7H 0J8

Thistledown Press gratefully acknowledges the financial assistance of the Canada Council for the Arts, the Saskatchewan Arts Board, and the Government of Canada through the Book Publishing Industry Development Program for its publishing program.

ALMON, BERT. "Starship Invaders", "The Warner Bros./Shakespeare Hour", "Driving Western Roads", "Look This Way Please" from *Deep North*, 1984; "For Nancy Going To War", "Southpaw's Paranoia" from *Blue Sunrise*, 1980. Reprinted by author's permission.

BARR, ALLAN. "Bed of Nails", "Say Something" from *The Chambered Nautilus*, 1992. Reprinted by author's permission.

BEARDSLEY, DOUG. "Rite of Passage", "The Perfect Poem", "Opus One" from *A Dancing Star*, 1988. Reprinted by author's permission.

BRETT, BRIAN. "Evolution in Every Direction" from *Evolution in Every Direction*, 1987. Reprinted by author's permission.

BUCKAWAY, CATHERINE. "The Souris Sings" from *Riding into Morning*, 1989. Reprinted by author's permission.

BUTTON, GREG. "In My Defence", "In the White Room" from *Inside of Midnight*, 1993. Reprinted by author's permission.

CAMPBELL, ANNE. "Oranges" from *Red Earth, Yellow Stone*, 1989; "Migraine", "Heart Exchange", "Elvis Sets It Free" from *Angel Wings All Over*, 1994. Reprinted by author's permission.

CATHERS, KEN. "Blue Heron", "As I Write This Down", "Rewrite", "Icarus" from *Sanctuary*, 1991. Reprinted by author's permission.

CAY, MARILYN. "Blue", "In the Pocket of Her Son's Jeans", "Pride", "To Daughter", "Seeding Time", "No Time for Mice", "Hometown Boy" from *Farm*, 1993. Reprinted by author's permission.

CHOYCE, LESLEY. "My Dog Watches Me Write a Poem", "On Becoming a Canadian Citizen" from *The Top of the Heart*, 1986. Reprinted by author's permission.

CHRISTENSEN, PETER. "Hail Storm", "Wasted Dolls", "Homecoming" from *Hail Storm*, 1977; "The Oil Rush Has Come" from *Rig Talk*, 1981;

"Mountain Rescue", "Chinook", "Transformation", "Pretending to Dance" from *To Die Ascending*, 1988. Reprinted by author's permission.

CLARK, JOHN LIVINGSTONE. "Existential Breakfast", "Gavin's Feet" from *Breakfast of the Magi*, 1994. Reprinted by author's permission.

COLLINS CHRIS. "Marks", "Duck Hunting", "Utopia Must Be Here — So Where are the Jobs?", "Kid Sky" from *Earthworks*, 1990. Reprinted by author's permission.

COOLEY, DENNIS. "You Take My Love" from *Dedications*, 1988. Reprinted by author's permission.

CROZIER, LORNA. "Trains", "Jewish Cemetery at Lipton", "Inner Space" from *Inside is the Sky*, 1976. Reprinted by author's permission.

CULLEN, MICHAEL. "South of Fort Macleod at a Buffalo Jump" from *The Curried Chicken Apocalypse*, 1979. Reprinted by author's permission.

DANIEL, LORNE. "In the Fold", "The Falls", "Bone Dance" from *Falling Together*, 1986. Reprinted by author's permission.

DILLOW, H.C. "Winter Mouse", "Mole" from *Orts and Scantlings*, 1984. Reprinted by author's permission.

DUBÉ, PAULETTE. "Pause During a Winter Sky", "L'Orage", "The Trees Dance Bare", "A Woman in a Portrait of Lace" from *The House Weighs Heavy*, 1992. Reprinted by author's permission.

GOM, LEONA. "Metamorphosis", "Blizzards", "The Way He Told It", "These Poems" from *Land of the Peace*, 1980; "Moved", "Widow", "Survival" from *Northbound*, 1984. Reprinted by author's permission and with the permission of Sono Nis Press, Vancouver.

GREEN, JIM. "Dead Horse Winter", "Drum Song" from *Beyond Here*, 1983. Reprinted by author's permission.

HAWLEY, HELEN. "Winds of My Country" from *Gathering Fire*, 1977. Reprinted by author's permission.

HICKS, JOHN V. "Wind in the Corn" from *Now is a Far Country*, 1978; "Dark Morning" from *Winter Your Sleep*, 1980; "Winter Zero", "Sonnet for a Small Girl" from *Sticks and Strings: Selected and New Poems*, 1988; "Payoff", "Snake",

"Town Spring" from *Month's Mind*, 1992; "Late Summer Weeds", "Felix", "Little Mouse", "Nativity" from *Overheard by Conifers*, 1996. Reprinted by author's permission.

HILL, GERALD. "Labour Day, Unemployed", "The Goaltender", "If Lafleur Never Plays Again", "The Mail Dog at Emma Lake" from *Heartwood*, 1985. Reprinted by author's permission.

HILLES, ROBERT. "My Father Waits", "After You Sleep I Sleep", "Stumblings", "This Poem Will Not Harm You" from *Outlasting the Landscape*, 1989. Reprinted by author's permission.

HILLIS, DORIS. "Idea for a Poem", "He Was 21" from *The Prismatic Eye*, 1985; "Daughters", "Stormhorses", "The Wait" from *Wheelings*, 1995. Reprinted by author's permission.

HORNE, LEWIS. "Watching My Daughters Drive Off for University" from *The Seventh Day*, 1982. Reprinted by author's permission.

HUNTER, BRUCE. "Slow Learner", "Snow Plow Driver's Dream", "For My Brother Daniel" from *Benchmark*, 1982; "June 23,1973", "Towards a Definition of Pornography", "Slow Learner" from *The Beekeeper's Daughter*, 1986. Reprinted by author's permission.

HYLAND, GARY. "The First Moon of Moose Jaw", "Elaine's Swimmers", "Telemachus" from *Just Off Main*, 1982; "The Doctor", "Sports Illustrated Photo", "A Safe and Easy Thing", "Out of Habit" from *After Atlantis*, 1991. Reprinted by author's permission.

JOHNSON, SHERRY. "Full Lunar Eclipse", "Psychotherapy" from *Pale Grace*, 1995. Reprinted by author's permission.

KEYS, WELDON. "For My Daughter", 1951. Reprinted by permission of University of Nebraska Press.

LANE, PATRICK. "[Magpie]", "[The line is doubtful]", "[Don't shake your hoary locks at me]", "[A bad line, breaking]" from *A Linen Crow, A Caftan Magpie*, 1984. Reprinted by author's permission.

LATTA, WILLIAM. "A Good Friday Birth" from *Summer's Bright Blood*, 1976. Reprinted by author's permission.

LEEDAHL, SHELLEY A. "When Summer Spreads", "Burning", "A Few Words for January", "Spring", "Mother Love", "Some Days All I Want from Life Is a Peanut Butter and Banana Sandwich" from *A Few Words for January*, 1990. Reprinted by author's permission.

LENT, JOHN. "Pastoral #1: St. Albert Sideroad, 1961" from *Frieze*, 1984; "Enclosed Garden, 1" from *The Face in the Garden*, 1990. Reprinted by author's permission.

LOWEY, MARK. "In the Field", "Sons of Icarus", "Icarus Revisited" from *Forgetting How To Fly*, 1987. Reprinted by author's permission.

MALTMAN, KIM. "Owls", "Elk On the Open Prairie", "Cafes" from *Branch Lines*, 1982. Reprinted by author's permission.

MARGOSHES, DAVE. "The Barber's Chair", "Arithmetic" from *Walking at Brighton*, 1988. Reprinted by author's permission.

McADAM, RHONA. "Hour of the Pearl", "Coming of Age on the Island", "White Dresses", "Domestic Hazard", "Moth Love", "Obscene Phone Calls" from *Hour of the Pearl*, 1987; "The Poem", "Animal Kingdom", "At Fifteen", "Money Talks", "Another Life to Live at the Edge of the Young and the Restless Days of Our Lives", "Coat of Many Poems" from *Creating the Country*, 1989; "Urban Renewal", "Country & Western" from *Old Habits*, 1993. Reprinted by author's permission.

MORTON, COLIN. "Pickled Watermelon", "My Father Writes a Poem Home from Europe", "Patching", "Spring Snow", "Empty Bottles" from *In Transit*, 1981. Reprinted by author's permission.

NISKALA, BRENDA. "Prairie Junk", "I Will Not Be the Grandmother" from *Ambergris Moon*, 1983. Reprinted by author's permission.

NOBLE, CHARLES. "Horse Around", "The Way the Mind Works" from *Afternoon Starlight*, 1984. Reprinted by author's permission.

ORMSHAW, PETER. "Picking Up Mom", "Cougars", "Shoes" from *The Purity of Arms*, 1993. Reprinted by author's permission.

POLSON, DON. "He Dies to Speak the Truth", "An April Lyric", "Autumn Rhyme", "December Twilight" from *Moving Through Deep Snow*, 1984. Reprinted by permission of the author's estate.

PURDY, AL. "Wilderness Gothic". Reprinted by author's permission.

RADISON, GARRY. "All There Is" from *White Noise*, 1982. Reprinted by author's permission.

REID, MONTY. "Skidooers", "The Disposal of Hazardous Wastes", "The Crochety Old Ladies Play Scrabble" from *The Life of Ryley*, 1981. Reprinted by author's permission.

RIVARD, KEN. "Humpbacks in the Sky", "Variables of My Father's Ambition", "Reliever", "Ice Time" from *Kiss Me Down To Size*, 1983. Reprinted by author's permission.

RUZESKY, JAY. "My Grandfather Was Offered a Contract with the Dodgers but My Grandfather's Father Offered Him the Farm and Said He Couldn't Have Both", "Learning to Smoke", "The One Right Girl in the World for You on the Streetcar Going by", "The Complete Poems of Mr. John Milton", "We Take Photographs" from *Am I Glad To See You*, 1992. Reprinted by author's permission.

SAPERGIA, BARBARA. "Firedance", "Coteau" from *Dirt Hills Mirage*, 1980. Reprinted by author's permission.

SCRIVER, STEVEN. "The Slap Shot", "Icarus" from *Between the Lines*, 1977. Reprinted by author's permission.

SIMISON, GREG. "My Family's Under Contract to Cancer", "Falling in Love", "Travesty", "West of Olds" from *Disturbances*, 1981. Reprinted by author's permission.

SORESTAD, GLEN. "Elegy for Sondra", "Faces" from *Ancestral Dances*, 1979; "Beer at Cochin" from *Prairie Pub Poems*, 1976; "Aide Mémoire", "Cat in Morning", "Fourteen", "Two Fish, One Morning", "Tunnels" from *West into Night*, 1991. Reprinted by author's permission.

STORY, GERTRUDE. "My Father Rode a Stallion", "The Worst Pain", "Crows" from *The Book of Thirteen*, 1981. Reprinted by author's permission.

STEVENSON, RICHARD. "Why Were All the Werewolves Men?" from *Why Were All the Werewolves Men?*, 1994. Reprinted by author's permission.

SUMMERHAYES, DON. "aide-mémoire", "The Onion Pickers" from *Heavy Horse Judging*, 1987. Reprinted by author's permission.

TIHANYI, EVA. "Urban Spell", "Elk Lake Imperative" from *Prophecies Near the Speed of Light*, 1984; "People Say She's Hyper", "My Mother Turns 50", "The Child Eventually Grows Up", "Prenatal Class" from *Saved by the Telling*, 1995. Reprinted by author's permission.

WAYMAN, TOM. "Metric Conversion", "Travelling Companions", "Wayman in Love", "Dead End" from *The Nobel Prize Acceptance Speech*, 1981. Reprinted by permission of author and of Harbour Publishing Co. Ltd., Madeira Park, British Columbia.

WEIS, LYLE. "The Mill Under His Skin", "An Open Letter to a Serious Writer", "Black Widow", "Icarus in the Okanagan", "Hawk in the Snow", "Vigil" from *The Mill Under His Skin*, 1992. Reprinted by author's permission.

WHIPPLE, GEORGE. "Innocence", "Indian Summer", "Astrophysics", "The Writing on the Wall", "Passing through Eden", "The Prodigal" from *Passing through Eden*, 1991. Reprinted by author's permission.

WREGGITT, ANDREW. "Eleanor, Fraser Lake", "Benediction", "At the Wedding", "Youngest in Canada", "Fishing" from *Man at Stellaco River*, 1985; "Sonny Liston", "Cars", "Burning My Father's Clothes" from *Making Movies*, 1989. Reprinted by author's permission.

The editors have reached into the literary archives of Thistledown Press to select and compile the poetry that is presented in this anthology. In a historical context these poems span the life of the press. Included in *In the Clear* is poetry that has been published over almost a quarter of a century by poets at every stage of their artistic development. Many of these poets are now among the very best writing contemporary Canadian poetry. However, *In The Clear* is not a chronicle of Thistledown Press' poetry publishing. It is an endeavour to bring back in print poetry that is as diverse in its concerns and craft as the poets, who come from all regions of Canada and beyond.

Many of the poems included in this anthology were selected because of "popular demand". Frequently they have been requested but unfortunately the collection in which they appeared was out of print. So like the music industry in the age of the compact disc, Thistledown Press decided that the time has come to give these poems a second life. In no way is the number of poems selected from the work of each poet intended to reflect the literary stature of the poet. The selection of the poems that make up *In the Clear* was done for one of many considerations — the distinctiveness of voice or craft; the evocativeness of geographic locale; the social and ecological concerns that confront people in this vast and diverse country.

In the Clear is an anthology of contemporary poetry that speaks with certainty and precision to the reader. Be it narrative or imagistic, the language is sincere and without artifice.

The poets in this anthology are arranged alphabetically. Two personal essays preface the poems while three meditations and numerous epigraphs are interspersed throughout the book. The intent is to create moments of provocation, reflection, or illumination that will enrich the reading experience. To assist the reader there is an alphabetized index of titles, an index of first lines, and a bibliography of each writer's poetry publications.

May your reading of *In the Clear* be an enriching and satisfying experience.

We thank the poets who so generously granted us permission to republish their poems.

— *The Editors*
August, 1998

Rhona McAdam

Like many poets, I live a divided life: one half earns money and the other writes poetry. Like many poets, I am my sole provider, meaning the earning half can, unless I'm careful, take priority.

I have not been careful in recent years, and the poetry-writing half of me is weeping in the background. The most often asked question by those who know I am more than the sum of my parts is "are you writing?" Alas, I am not.

I lead a busy life in an interesting, demanding and lucrative job. The conventional, non-poetry-writing world not only under-stands but positively approves of my throwing myself into my work. The job easily dominates my life and leaves me no time or energy to write. It leaves me no time or energy to read poetry or go to readings or send poems to magazines or even talk about poetry with my friends, who are also busy with the rest of their lives. But that is only half an answer.

A few people at work know that I write poetry. They are interested by this fact, it makes me something of a novelty, but they would never view it as a serious sideline. Were I published by a big commercial publisher, were I reviewed in the *Times Literary Supplement* or some similar heavyweight publication, this might be different. But I am published by a small press nobody outside the literary, nay the poetry world, has heard of; I am reviewed in magazines whose names mean nothing to the readers-of-the-*Times* who surround me; I perform at venues someone who does not follow poetry would never have heard of.

In short, I am your average poet. And for your average poet, the rest of the world views my art as a hobby, something their daughters might have done in their adolescence but which serious people do not pursue, particularly if it does not pay money.

I think back to the time I was writing. What was different? Well, I was younger. When you are in your twenties and even thirties, single, childless, you have a world of time in front of you.

If you put the serious stuff off and take odd and interesting jobs to pay the rent while you write and be literary in the other parts of your life, nobody bats an eye. If you are gaining from this experience, so much the better.

You can carry on this way quite happily for years. You can do all the things you need to stimulate your writing: take workshops, hang out with poets, attend poetry readings, read lots of poetry books and magazines. It all helps, it all keeps you tuned to the music necessary for writing.

But one day you hit a personal milestone. You find you know people not so much older than you who have run into career problems they never anticipated, whose health suddenly goes wrong, whose mortgages overtake them, whose families need attention and money, and you start paying attention to all those boring words like "security" and "pension" and worst of all "career". You are forced to realise you too have a shelf life and that nothing can be taken for granted. It may distract you from your writing; it will certainly force you to realise that your crowd is changing and the world of poetry has become more distant.

Distant, but not gone. Not completely. Every so often I wander back in, or am invited, or am dragged in by kindly friends. I find myself renewed, reminded that I have something outside my job, something which defines me permanently, that will last beyond the fickle world of employment.

A colleague at work told me that when he left his salaried job to do contract work with our company, he was shocked to realise his friends from work were no longer there for him. And how many of your friends at work will you keep when you eventually leave your job, once the office chat isn't there to give you a common interest and a topic of conversation?
Poetry is real and it lasts.

A friend of mine in England, raised in a working class council estate, said the class system disappeared for him in poetry. It's true that in the arts in Britain, everyone in a similar genre is on an equal footing, finally judged by talent alone; that's rare.

Every so often I am able to write, a little, and I am invigorated and cleansed by getting the words into a poem; it channels and settles my thoughts. Every so often someone recognises my name from my poetry and tells me so, and I realise it matters, it matters to me that someone was moved by my words. These are the things that make it worthwhile.

Lately I have been asking myself how I can return to the world of words, and here are my answers, which I am going to staple to my forehead. Maybe they will help others lost on the periphery:

Go to readings. Nothing inspires me like a poetry reading. The music of the words, the images that haunt the air after the poet sits down. After a powerful reading, I always wish there were an enforced period of silence to let all those words ricochet round the room before we start talking.

Read the best. Read people you've never heard of. Browse the shelves of libraries, bookstores, secondhand dealers. Read people from other countries! Read anthologies, the more obscure the better; follow the trail of a poet encountered in a quote or allusion.

Play with languages. I have limited — very limited! — French. Undeterred by my own ignorance, I will sometimes read poetry in French. Even if I don't understand it all, it's still possible to catch a glimmer of the light that runs through a poem. Try translating — I use the word loosely — into English: I find that what little I understand can help me jump off into a parallel line.

Play games. There are so many games that can be used as leaping off points for poems: make some up! Be surreal: use words on bits of paper, or the fridge magnets, to string random images together. Make a poem using the old colour/emotion/taste/sound contrivance. Read obscure dictionaries — of proverbs, of odd words — and use them for poem topics.

What else? If you lack discipline, borrow a taskmaster. Go to a workshop. Crack those dusty notebooks. Write. Write. Write!

London, 1998

JUGULAR MUSIC

Patrick Friesen

These are a handful of thoughts and feelings about poetry, its place, its process. Poetry is dear to me. I grew up with it, in one form or another. Ballads, poems, the Bible, Schubert, hymns. It's a way of thinking, a way of being. It's life blood. Jugular music.

Certainly in poetry there has not been very much that has seized me in some time. Too much of it is unmusical, unfelt, at best a cleverness. Much of it doesn't matter to me.

So, how to begin. With the feel. The interrelatedness of everything. I take my cues from music. Rhythm and image. I look for the feel. Poetry begins there, I think, in human feeling. That's where the fire is lit.

It's lit in the child, that wide-eyed wonder; then it's doused as we're formed into citizens; and often, it glows again in old age. Direct experiences. No self-censorship, fearless.

New music happens when there's a need, not when someone decides it's time. This century jazz had to happen, given the complexity of cultural realities in the United States. Untutored formally, it took elements from the past, including ragtime, gospel, and blues, and went in a new direction, growing into its own depth, through swing and improvisation into bebop and beyond. It became something different when critics wrote about it, explained it.

Rock, too, had to happen. Again, untutored, felt out of a web of religion and culture, tearing free of these to a degree, flaming brightly. Then possessed by the producers, the money people. They try to perpetuate it, start new trends, create new stars. Sometimes, it makes them a lot of money, but there's no depth, no staying power.

People still listen to Louis Armstrong and Charlie Parker, Presley, the Beatles. The moment of ecstasy that each was, the feel.

I'm listening to a CD of Elvis Presley's Sun Sessions. These are the very first records he made, before he achieved fame and a slow distintegration into cult religious status. By today's standards these records are almost primitively recorded. There is, however, something absolutely fresh, exciting, energetic, emotional, humourous, and true about these early records. "That's Alright Mama" sounds guileless. Simple human expression on a popular level.

Charlie Parker, essentially self-taught, finding out at his first jam in Kansas City that there was more than one key to play in. Going home to learn all the keys. If he'd listened, he would have found he only needed three or four keys. He taught himself all twelve. Changing jazz forever with his improvising, his search for the "feel" in each song he played.

Or, listen to Sandy Denny, Van Morrison and Richard Manuel singing "Tura Lura". Listen to an old scratchy record of the Spanish singer of Canto Jondo, La Nina De Los Peines, singing "Saeta". Listen to yodelling or Sonny Rollins playing his saxaphone's mouthpiece only on "East Broadway Rundown", terrifyingly human. Uilleann pipes with a tin whistle, "Amazing Grace" by almost anyone, or Glenn Gould humming human imperfection among the precise notes of "The Goldberg Variations".

Unselfconscious and felt.

Like childhood. Like the best of our art, our poetry. Something direct, unmediated, body to body, tongue to ear, human breath. Something so honest that even if you don't understand all of it, you trust it, you listen because you know you *can* understand it. Besides, you are understanding at a non-analytical, non-verbal level. Absorbing it, body and mind.

In contrast, a possibly apocryphal story: a musician told me recently that Schoenberg reached a point where he said he could no longer explain his music, so he quit playing and composing. Theory, the intellect, explanation, seen as the only legitimate source of art. The labyrinth of intellect. Is this what Milton called hell? The intellect, like the actor staring into a mirror, enamoured of itself, becoming convinced it's the only reality.

Phillip Larkin wrote in a letter: "The only worthwhile theories, or statements of belief, are works of art. All else is just farting Annie Laurie through a keyhole as Gulley Jimson says." And the novelist John Gardner, "Intellect is the chief distractor of the mind."

Theory has its place. In the cart behind the horse. Or, as Tom Stoppard observed: "It is a mistake to assume that my plays are the end product of ideas. The ideas are the end product of the plays."

All writers work with ideas, experiment with form, but they don't neccessarily build intellectual cathedrals. Critics and theorists look for patterns and consistencies in literature. They look for what holds together, what doesn't, from that particular point of view. This can be interesting, even valuable, for readers and writers. As long as it keeps its place as a reflective analysis exploring, in its limited fashion, what has already been written. Even then, in the hands of those with some power within the writing community at large, it can wreak havoc with those poets not belonging to the right church.

Some people need theory as an ideology, an intellectual construct that explains things to them, not only things they don't understand otherwise, but things they don't seem to want to understand on any level but the intellectual. And they need to control, dominate the field. There's an astonishing narrowness of thought here they don't recognize. A narrowness of interpretation and imagination.

Reminding me of the minor theological differences among some of the churches in my hometown. One church argued that to be properly baptized you had to be dunked in a tank or some shallow river. Another church countered with the sufficiency of sprinkling on the crown of the head. In fact, the Essenes, who apparently first baptized believers, would hold a person's head under water to the point of losing consciousness and possibly dying. The full experience of death by water and the possible visions of an oxygen-starved brain.

Dunking or sprinkling. The pale theories go on. The building of cathedrals. And, then, the question of who gets in, who doesn't. Who decides? Some academics, said Doris Lessing in a radio interview, think they hold the keys to literature. No one cometh to the literature but by them. As one such academic said to me after I mentioned how much I, and the rest of the audience, had enjoyed a Leonard Cohen concert, "the trouble with Cohen is that he gives all those fans the impression they know something about poetry." The great unwashed.

One may or may not like Cohen, may or may not know much about poetics, no problem there; it's the arrogance and elitism of this "holder of the keys" attitude that is a real threat to poetry. The distancing of poetry from people. The steady elimination of the emotional, the feeling, aspect of poetry. The reduction of poetry to a theoretical game, a game that may well keep them busy and employed.

Thinking that we should be glad for Cohen, how he's taken poetry back to what it was originally, song; how he's made it accessible to more people. When theory imposes itself on literature, when writers begin to write according to the theory they've bought into, a kind of death has begun. This is not to deny change — that happens in spite of us — but it is to deny the domination of arbitrary theories held by a relatively small number of people who do indeed hold some keys, not to literature, but to positions of power and influence.

Ideology dies. Poetry, so far, hasn't. In countries dominated by tyrannies, time and again, people survived physically because they survived spiritually. Often this was because of poetry; not its theoretical form but, at its best, its balance of intellect and feeling. Its music.

Marina Tsvetaeva and Anna Akhmatova in the Soviet Union. Highly intelligent poets writing out of a harmony of mind and heart, body and soul. Yes, engaging in literary arguments, but always the whole human writing to the whole human listening.

An immediacy. A need to write, and a need to hear. Human stories, human emotions and thoughts. Accessible words.

Poets and words. Trying to use words to explore and communicate the ancient, never-ending human concerns, joys and humours, directly and freshly. Intelligence, not intellect. As in the 19th century Russian intelligentsia, where intellectualism was not necessary to belong; an unschooled poet whose verses moved common people could be included. We, too, though our society and culture are different from that of the old Soviet Union, can atrophy.

I'll listen to Nina Simone voicing despair in "Ne Me Quitte Pas". I'll take the intellegence of the Bill Evans trio playing "Solar" at the Village Vanguard. And Gwendolyn MacEwen reciting from the *T.E. Lawrence Poems* at Mary Scorer Bookstore in Winnipeg in 1983.

Accessible poetry. Imagery and music, comparisons, relationships. Thought and feeling. A poem does not have to be explained. It speaks for itself. It says exactly what it means. It isn't philosophy, theology, economics, literary theory, or politics in fancy clothes. All these things may exist within poems, but they don't explain the poem.

The poem has to have an emotional component, a rhythmic component. It must appeal to more than the intellectual aspect of human beings, be more than a page exercise. It doesn't worry about contradictions, has no need to become a theory. Poetry gestates. It uses language, with all its resonance, to attempt to understand the whole human in the natural world, in the world humanly created, in the intersections between the two. It explores, reveals, weeps, praises.

Poetry, for me, has a quality of what D.H. Lawrence called "in-betweenness". It lives between the lines and lies. It straddles intellect and emotion. It is interested in what falls in the cracks, not necessarily in what receives attention. It keeps alive what is being forgotten.

A stone, a reed. The hum, in wintertime, of a powerline crossing the snowdrifts on my grandfather's farm. These are things I remember, things I know, in a way.

For me, poetry is always knowing, never knowledge. Giving voice. Evoking, invoking. Holding together loosely. Precise. Elusive. A handful of water.

I'm tired of seeing poems with endless brackets and parentheses breaking compound words into their component parts. I know how words are constructed. I'm bored by writers reminding me that they're writing the book I'm reading. I'm tired of not only literary theory being imposed on poetry but, also, the theories of various social and political causes.

Ethnicity, gender, and theories of feminism, postmodernism, poststructuralism, postcolonialism, etc. If any of these things are carried within the larger poem, fine; to hell with them when they issue marching orders to the poet or the reader. Theory becomes ideology. Ideology kills. Resistant to theory? Damn right.

Poetry undermines and sabotages authority simply by existing. It resists categorization and manipulation. It comes from nowhere and goes nowhere. A moment of process that gives voice to what is voiceless.

I love the simplicity of a Japanese haiku. Or the diary entry of an unimportant person. Chekov's father wrote: "A peony blossomed in the garden. Maria Petrovna came. The peony faded. Maria Petrovna left."

Simplicity and freshness. The words of an amateur. I love to hear the guitarist's fingers on the fretboard, I love to hear the poet's breath. I love to hear them work. Watching the dance form backstage. Direct, not self-censoring. Perhaps we need the amateur again. The amateur poet. Something felt and intelligent and expressed in a form true to that feel. A balance. And a trust in our personal experiences.

Saul Bellow said in a recent interview: " . . . There have been tremendous mistakes in thought, but the worst of all was the casting out of all connection with one's own nature and one's own knowledge. Private knowledge has in it a rare kind of truth."

Enough quotes. Even in quoting these various artists I am falling back on what we're taught to do: appeal to authority. Why not simply speak out of personal experience? Authority doesn't make anything more true. There is, I guess, a reassurance in quoting other artists, a feeling of not being alone. And, often, there is the pleasure of hearing one's thoughts expressed more beautifully by others. Like Charlie Parker spontaneously quoting someone else's composition within one of his. The fun of it, the endless interrelatedness of things.

I don't know. But I do. I know what works for me. You know what works for you. Not cleverness, but the truth you know when you hear it, read it. The truth of your wide-awake, unafraid intelligence. The poetry that speaks fully to you.

I'm not saying all writing, all poets, are equally good. Not at all; they're not. The writing of poetry may be a democratic activity. The creation of an excellent poem is not. I believe poetry is a calling. But you've got to find that out. It isn't announced with trumpets. And if you become a good poet, it doesn't place you on a pedestal. You have your work, that's all. You are not a brain surgeon with a steady hand, nor are you a slick second-baseman turning a double play. You are not a cultural worker. You are a poet.

You have to remain accessible. Not simplistic, not stupid, not some versifier. Accessible. Speaking well, poetically. Not writing in the stratosphere, but not writing down to people either. Coming through and being heard.

Writing as prayer, an interior conversation with god knows whom. With the numerous selves I am? The Lord? Who's that? What I know is when I was young, a first-time father, and my six-month-old daughter in a high fever, I feared. I hadn't yet learned the experienced parent's nonchalance. I held her to my bare chest; I was cooler by far than she was, and she found it comforting. When she finally fell asleep, I went to my room to write a poem. It was literally a prayer for my child. It wasn't written to be published; in fact, I destroyed it once she was well. It was a prayer to the greater power I knew firsthand. Letting go, giving it over to whatever/whoever it was I talked with when I wrote. In the process, as always, I found a stillness.

I've always had these interior conversations, since I was a child. Later, they became poems. I don't know who I speak with, but it's intimate; there is knowing back and forth. This conversation is only possible if I let go into the process and, I believe, if I don't name the other. Once you explain and name, it's gone. That's how it works, always has. As a poet, I let go to the world, its objects, and am possessed by them. Then I can write. As an Anabaptist theologian said long ago, "comprehending the invisible through the visible". In the end, it seems, we all have to let go of the world that has been an utter presence all our lives. That is an awesome loss. Or, maybe not. I'll find out.

There is mystery in the world, in the spirit, in poetry. There are, among the hours of tough work, moments of inspiration. Why deny this? Why fear it? And yet it is denied. Poetry is nothing but learning the right tricks in schools, in workshops? Bullshit. Can anyone become an excellent athlete, a fine surgeon, as long as he or she gets the right training? Obviously not.

Throughout history there has been an acceptance of inspiration, of firsthand knowing of it. Receiving the ghost. Inhalation. The word covers a lot of human experience.

I've used words that are considered unacceptable by some. *Mystery, spirit, inspiration, prayer.* You can add *heart* and *soul.* For many people they have meaning. The words are undoubtedly misused, used superficially, but they stand. And what they represent, in one's personal experience, stands.

Like the Essenes' baptisms, poetry, whether humourous or serious, is life and death stuff. It shifts perceptions, changes lives. Jugular music.

In the face of certain moments, death, let's say, or birth, love, a piece of music, or simply stillness, all theories, the complexities and labyrinths of self-circling intellectuality, fall away. Suddenly, there is only the clarity and simplicity of the newly born, the dying, the naked yearning human spirit.

Poetry is powerless. Like the child, or old age. Unencumbered. Answering to no authority. Poetry, at its best, brings light.

Vancouver, 1998

Abridged from a lecture presented at the eighth annual Caroline Heath Memorial Lecture, November 1, 1996 in Saskatoon.

No civilized society has ever managed to do entirely without poetry — the writing or the reading of it. Poets go about their business as if this fact never occurs to them, and so they should. Poetry is rooted in such ironies, and it's from the simultaneous acceptance of contradictory ideas that art arises.

— Allan Barr

Everything is poetry. In the beginning was the word, and the word made us. It gave us our history and our recorded knowledge. The "intense language" that poetry is has been often scorned, yet it survives, and will continue to survive in its many variations, each generation singing its own song.

— Brian Brett

Poetry gives your most intimate self the chance to talk to the most intimate self of another. When these two meet the sparks fly, the poem is charged with light, and a new way of seeing and saying enters the world.

Every time you pay attention, you praise. When that praise is uttered in a voice that is your own, it may become a poem.

— Lorna Crozier

Patrick Lane

What we reach for is our voice, that strange utterance that is entirely our own and which we cannot recognize because it sounds like no other we have heard or read. Poetry grows out of poetry, language out of language. We grow our vocabularies out of the rich earth that is the sound our mothers and fathers made when we lay in our cribs and listened to the simplicity of song. But it is not only the accumulation of words with their many resonant and hidden meanings that we take for our own. We take structures as well, the forms of speech and song. Why do we construct the poems we do? Why is the made thing on the page or in our ears unique to us and us alone? And perhaps there is no answer to that and we must take the form and content of our lives and accept them in the faith that what we make is ourselves. But that self, unique and absolute, is always a part of the community from which we arise. That which is common to you is common to all and the well-made poem or story is a reflection of the community's concerns of which you are only a single facet.

The difficulty for the young writer is to have faith that, through constant practise, the good poem will emerge. I have said that the time spent finding a way to speak, the hours, weeks, and years of practising upon the instrument of language, is no different than trying to command the endless complex nuances that a violin or flute offers. I have called the hours we spend reading and writing *piano exercises* and so they are. What is the story you want to tell, and is that the question you must ask yourself, for surely, if you dream of someday becoming a good writer then you know in your heart you have a story and it *must* be told or you will die, not physically perhaps, but spiritually. The harder question you must ask yourself is, *What way will I tell it?* for surely it is the way the story is told that holds the reader or listener to the song. Whenever I am in doubt about the felicity of my own voice, my ability to place a perception on the page, I turn to the masters for I know they are the greatest teachers. We choose to be writers and artists because we believe, as Gwendolyn MacEwen said in her poem "Dark Pines Under Water", *there is something down there and it wants to be told*. The great masters are those who have achieved perfection of form. There is not a single word you can change in Ezra Pound's "Exile's Letter" to make it better than it is. A line such as Theodore Roethke's "She moved in circles and those circles moved", is as perfect and mysterious to me today as it was when I first read it in 1967.

It is to achieve something as perfect as this in our own poetry that we write. We go back to the masters to be reminded of how difficult it is and will be to achieve an equal greatness. We go to them to be reminded of how humble is our effort, yet we persist, else why continue at all? *Where is the voice coming from?* Rudy Wiebe asked that question and the answer is, nowhere but ourselves. Persist. e.e.cummings said, "If after ten years of hard work you have written one good line of poetry then you can consider that you have begun." Robert Lowell told Anne Sexton, when she gave him a seventeen-line poem she had written, "That's a marvellous poem, Anne. Now scrap the first sixteen lines and begin with the last line." Those seem harsh words, but they are words from two twentieth century masters. It is not a futile endeavour you have chosen for yourselves, but is a long, hard road you have chosen. That choice required bravery on your part, as well as audacity and something akin to foolhardiness, but if the story is there, in you, then you *must* be a writer for every story needs telling. How you tell it is the question. Where does it begin? Once upon a time, and the child closes his eyes and listens and the words he hears are what become of him.

Bert Almon was born in East Texas. He was educated at the
University of Texas at El Paso and the University of New Mexico.
He came to Canada in 1968 to teach in the English Department at
the University of Alberta and has lived in Edmonton ever since.
He has been publishing books of poetry for three decades.

STARSHIP INVADERS

What do the hot-knifers and coke-sniffers know?
His habit is dropping quarters in the slot
and taking the levers, watching the starships
blink onto the screen, nine in rows of three,
then peel off row by row toward his planet.
He sends bright dots — laser torpedoes — against them,
erases each ship in a shower of flashes
to win the first match. The second speeds up,
the third he usually loses, the one that wins
a free game. Lunch money, paper route
and allowance go down the slot, so after hours
he has a job sweeping up the arcade
to earn a little more. In the back room
there's still a gaudy pinball machine
used by older people, but he despises
the materiality of it: the steel ball
rolling through baffles, the flippers
and buzzers. Starship Invaders is clean,
silent, a dance among printed circuits.
He has no time for lunches, for girls
and cars. This is pure, mind against the mind
of the machine. In his daydreams, the hands
moving at the controls are flashing lights.

THE WARNER BROS./SHAKESPEARE HOUR

"Will you walk out of the air, my lord?"

The fine tuning won't prevent
channel 4 from drifting into 3
as a faint background
so that *Hamlet* is haunted
by ghostly figures
of the Coyote and the Roadrunner

As Hamlet says *"To be or not to be"*
I can make out the Coyote climbing
a ladder suspended in mid-air
Convention says he won't fall
until he tops the ladder and looks down
He'll smash on the desert floor
and come back renewed in another frame

Hamlet finishes his soliloquy
and greets the fair Ophelia
The Coyote has built a bomb
and lights the fuse
He has no trouble taking arms
while Hamlet is the man who looks down
and knows that resurrection
is not a convention of his play
We share his terror
rung by rung

DRIVING WESTERN ROADS

Saskatchewan 14

What makes this grey and yellow autumn
unendurable isn't the dried thistles
in the right of way nor the rusted cars
by old farmhouses shedding their shingles
It's the one thin donkey intently grazing
in what looks like a field of bare earth

Local Attractions

Wainwright had the world's biggest buffalo
but I couldn't see it from the bus
so I can't say if it was alive or dead

Cut Knife had the world's biggest tomahawk
The Indians in front of the pool hall surely knew
where it's kept but the bus drove right past them

The world's biggest decorated easter egg
can be seen from the road at Vegreville
Keep your eyes on the stripe and you'll miss it

No Stopping on Shoulder

Passing through Hillsboro
we saw a fence full of morning glories
their faces open to the east
We gave them just the right interval —
some splendors should be glimpsed —
by dropping down to second gear
then easing back to third and fourth
We knew that the sun they faced
would be waiting for us in the west

LOOK THIS WAY PLEASE

A red light means the camera is on

The only trouble with the medium
is that it makes everything medium
Coming to honour poetry I am given
ten minutes between the ten minutes each
for Home Security and Fitness Fun

The police can show six basic locks
each mounted in a section of door
They caution against paranoia
but point out all the dangers
While I'm digging in the garden
someone could be in the living room
My paranoia goes them one farther
If I'm in the living room
someone could be in the garden
pulling up unsecured radishes

In my ten minutes I show books
that open freely on their hinges
I'm treated with great courtesy
but don't stay for Fitness Fun
I pick my way out over the cables
Poetry is not breaking and entering
It is a message slipped under the door
You don't even have to read it
It wants to tell you about danger
life and death and good parties
A message slipped under your door

ten above on Boxing Day
a break in the cold
I drove south to Calgary
              a girl and her police dog
              snow currents swirling over their feet
              good company for a sleepy driver

the girl was Nancy
              just over eighteen and wearing
"one pair of tights
long underwear
two pairs of pants
two sweaters
one scarf
one parka
and it turned out warm"

the dog was Maggie
              ten months old and wearing

her own fur
           sleeping peacefully on the floor
           soft snout benign against my foot

we fogged up the windows with talk
Nancy wiped them with her scarf
                everything was far-out
she wrote down the books I mentioned
on the flyleaf of *The Prophet*
              notebook addressbook and Bible
"You've read it?
         it's so beautiful

you've read *The Little Prince?*

             far-out

do you eat brown rice?
did you know meat is poison?

             what I like is doing acid
             running out of the house
             hugging the first person I see
             far-out"

she took off the parka and one sweater

             relief in the stuffy car
"do you like going naked?

             it's so natural
you forget some people don't like it
you can even get arrested
it's like a real war sometimes
but we'll win   we've got love
they can't fight that"

             then it was the crossroads
             she put on the sweater and parka
             said thank you and got out

I left her standing on the shoulder
thumbing her way to the free life on the coast
or an asteroid with a magic flower

the hip middle class calls it the Children's Crusade
says far-out with a straight face
not remembering any history

             but I've met enough pirates
             and slave merchants on the road
to wish Nancy had more armor
and Maggie was a little fiercer

             Edmonton/Calgary, December 26, 1970

SOUTHPAW'S PARANOIA

Growing up lefthanded.
you always feel wrong
the bad penmanship
a signed confession

Going to Miss Slaughter
for extra practice
she sighed and said
"You never learned to print
why should you practice script?
I tried to teach your mother
she was lefthanded too"

Or the doctor dipping
gauze into plaster
"Aren't you lucky
it's just the left arm
a nasty break like this"

And the years of botchery
with scissors and canopeners
meant for Righty
and the guitar manuals
you have to read backward
there are skills in life
you'll never master
rules in life
you never understand
until you get it all wrong
"Hey, you can't do it that way"
from the eternal shop teacher

There's your mother's saying
"If you're not careful
one of these mornings
you'll wake up dead"
a lefthanded maxim
if you've ever heard one —

Poets create, they make something, and often the "poem-truth" reveals some aspect of the human experience and the human condition that transcends and transforms our lives.

— Doug Beardsley

Allan Barr was born in Shaunavon, Saskatchewan, and educated at the University of Saskatchewan. He began his writing career in Saskatoon and is a former editor of *Grain*. He has lived for the last ten years in Cumberland, British Columbia, where he works in a sawmill.

SAY SOMETHING

So they come into the Broadway Café, this perfect couple. He's got the button-down and the pleats and important hair. He looks like a man of substance as they used to say. She's an earth-mother type, denim from neck to ankle and serious brown boots. All I can see of her hair is a glossy black band high across her forehead. The rest of it's wrapped in a red-and-white bandanna. Where the bandanna's knotted at the nape of her neck rides a heavy bundle of red-and- white-covered hair. A few strands have escaped from the bundle and the light coming in through the front window catches those strands floating around her like we're all in some movie.

They get their cheesecake, Grand Marnier for him and hers is Amaretto, and they both have raspberry sauce and café au lait. I watch them trading tastes. They don't feed each other, they are mature and decorous people, but the way she slides her fork edge-first through his dessert makes me hungry just watching. It takes them a hell of a long time to eat, and when they finish they get refills of coffee. Her mouth leaves no stain of lipstick on the white pottery mug.

It's clear that they've settled in for a while, there's no way I can outwait them. One of the things I've lost lately is patience. So I fold up my newspaper and leave money on the table and try to slide sideways out of the café.

She sees me anyway. He looks up, curious at the recognition in her look, and I am frozen, locked between the eyes of this perfect couple. After an hour or two she figures she has to say something.

Ed, she says, this is Paul. From work. Paul, my husband Ed.

He looks me over. There are times you just have to be brave, so I stick my open, empty hand out in front of me. Glad to meet you, Paul, I say.

BED OF NAILS

My wife comes home from work one day and says we've got to get ourselves a bed of nails. They're all the rage on the coast. She keeps up with this stuff, which is how we got those crystals a while ago, and the Thai cooking utensils before that. She doesn't steer us wrong very often, though I had to tell her that the green para-chute-silk harem pants weren't flattering on a woman her age.

Anyway I'm a little suspicious about this bed of nails business. I went years without a decent sleep, through the waterbed thing and the futon thing. Then the magazines started to talk about cocooning and my wife went out and got us a Sealy Posturepedic. Put it right in the middle of the living room. We liked that bed so well that we cocooned right through the homeless thing, where you were supposed to go sleep on newspapers over a sewer grate or something.

Now she says that cocooning's out and the homeless thing's out and what we need is a bed of nails. But honey, I say, won't it ruin the Eurodown? She just shakes her head at me. Says that the bed of nails gets you centred, concentrating, restful. I point out that the crystals were supposed to get us centred, and the pyramid too. Now they're just more stuff to be dusted.

She's got her heels dug in about this, though, and the more I think about it the more this bed of nails starts to grow on me. I can see the upside, as we used to say in our BMW phase. A little restful concentration in bed might be just the thing to get me centred. Plus there's the possibility of veils and saris and some of this Kama Sutra stuff, and there hasn't been too much of that going on in our Posturepedic.

Honey, I say, I guess I could warm up to this idea. She doesn't waste any time. Whips out a four-colour brochure and dials the toll-free number that minute.

I never knew her to be fickle before, but she gave up on that bed pretty quick. Said it made her itchy. And those other practices I was thinking about, that stuff never did come to pass. Fact is, she hasn't been around much lately. I believe she's found some other kind of bed that's more her speed. Like the Magic Fingers at the Travelodge.

I don't mind that too much. I'm used to this bed now, it's been weeks since I even tried to get out of it. If she was to come back now I don't think I could get up to help her with her bags or anything. But I guess you'd have to say I still love her. I know I'll always keep a space for her. Right here beside me.

Doug Beardsley was born in Montreal. Educated at the University of Victoria and York University, he has taught English at a number of Canadian and foreign schools, and currently resides in Victoria where he teaches at the University of Victoria. He has published prolifically since 1976.

RITE OF PASSAGE

Father, when I stole
Three comics at age twelve
I'd no intention of growing up
A thief. I knew I'd done wrong
But the desire was too great,
And though I'd money
In my pocket, this was
A mathematics I made
Sense of; a childlike passion
To have these books and be free

To buy others and have more.
Not paying for them I paid
Too high a price, shaming you
And all you stood for
In your own store. That night
I sent myself to bed
With no supper, stayed awake
Knowing you'd come to my room
To punish me. I still see
Your painful mouth quivering

Over me: 'Why did you do it,
Say you're sorry'; feel how

my arms ached holding them
Bent back at the elbow
So you could slap them
With your soft palms.
Before I fall
Asleep you hold my head
To your belt buckle:
We both feel better, weeping.

THE PERFECT POEM

What I wish
to write
is not here
but somewhere
beyond.

What I make
is a poem,
a small house
to live in,
a holiday resort.

What I see
is the shape
I try to read,
a perfect
waterfall of words.

What I dream
is the same
poem I make
but I always
wake up.

OPUS ONE

The silver spoon
                    percussive
                              mahogany music

you make is far from
                    accidental
                              it is

pure sound
          found in nature
                    & your face

delights
          in the joy you make
                    when you create such a

racket
          you might call music
                    if you were old enough

to speak
          & could say
                    I am here

& didn't have to
          beat your silvery
                    baton

like some carved bone
          against my incredulous
                    ear

Born in Vancouver, Brian Brett studied literature at Simon Fraser University. He has been writing, editing, and publishing since the 1960s. He is both a poet and fiction writer who has published several books in each genre. Brett lives on a farm on Salt Spring Island, British Columbia.

EVOLUTION IN EVERY DIRECTION

The ribs of the dead trees broke against the sky above the spit, and vast, cumulus clouds raced the sun to the horizon. We launched the boat, my father and I, and steered into the sky just beyond the spit. The big water was still, slow despite the life that flashed beneath us, out of sight and hungry.

Rebecca Spit. Not many had discovered it then. We camped alone by the sandy beach, stuffing ourselves with clams, oysters, and the huckleberries that grew in the deep wood. But most of all, we came for the bluebacks, those small coho salmon that rushed through the waters of the strait every June. They travelled in huge schools, their fins boiling the water when they surfaced.

Throughout the week we trolled under sunrise and sunset skies; then the dogfish arrived, seeping into the bay overnight, and our lines fought only these small sharks. They took bait, they took Tom Macks, they even took Flashtails on the surface. We fished shallow for the cohos, with four ounces of lead, sometimes less. If we felt lucky we'd shift deep and try for spring salmon, but there wasn't a chance with the dogfish striking. Our fishing turned into carnage as

we destroyed whatever we caught. Once, we hooked a
coho and a dogfish came up behind, leaving us only a
head attached to the hook.

My father hated these deep pests . . . mudsharks,
dogfish: they stripped your bait, bent your hooks,
snapped your lines, devoured, scoured the ocean
bottom like quick vacuums with teeth. Everything
has its place, but some things have no place with
fishermen, especially dogfish. There was a war here,
and we lost. Twenty years ago the ocean was still
endless.

It was a killing day. I bludgeoned and slit open
too many sharks, dumping the entrails over the side,
watching the carnivores, still alive, devour their own
guts. They are difficult to kill, a simple blow is never
enough.

At last the mountains covered the sun and my
cursing father steered the boat back to camp. No
salmon lay at our feet, only one giant shark which we
hadn't bothered to slit and return to the sea.
Exhausted by the day's murders, we beached as the
last red followed the sun into darkness. A big hook
dragged the night over our heads, and the moon
followed like one of those slow sharks looking for the
rip. The broken trees at the spit's end, funereal, cast
an eeriness, reminding me of Indian graveyards and
the strange fears that follow men into forests.

My disgusted father limped up the beach, stiff
and angry, leaving me the bloodied skiff. I flipped out
the five foot shark and used sea water to wash away
the gore in the boat. Tomorrow, we'd try again.

Sometimes we break our patterns. I had slit and
hurled two dozen sharks into the sea during the past
few days, always by the tail, avoiding the sharp spike

in the dorsal fin. This one I grabbed by the
midsection and picked off the sand to wheel it around
into the sea; but I squeezed. My hands became
someone else's hands, sensitive to the life. Something
came out with a gentle pop, and it was alive, a shark
from the belly of the shark. I dropped the dead
mother, and stared at the small replica squirming in
the sand.

I picked up the shark . . . dirty and almost dead it
wriggled in my hand, yolk sac still attached. Then I
slid the shark into the shallows where it lay quiet for
a moment; it shivered and swam a short, slow
distance before it turned and settled to the bottom,
watching me — cold blooded, accusing. Only five
inches long and already aware of where it belonged,
what its life was. I returned to the corpse of the
mother. When I'd finished milking her womb, six of
the sharks swam the shallows, their tiny eyes
glowing like emerald pins in the moonlight; they were
looking for the great green stretch ahead. Then they
were gone. I hurled the carcass of the mother after
them; perhaps she'd be their first meal.

At camp, I said nothing as I sat down to a dinner
of yesterday's salmon stuffed with huckleberries and
baked over the fire. The night was good. The moon
poured its silver on us; we were unearthly figures by
the fire, throwbacks, savages from another time
devouring the flesh of the sea. And I was wilder than
any. Something deep had been driven into me, had
gaffed my bloodstream. I'd taken innocent life, and
given a bit of it back. My brain was more simple,
swam on a stem of streamlined, uncomplicated
nerves. My teeth were longer and sharper when they
sank into the meat of the salmon. I was cartilage
instead of bone. My hand, evolved from a finny

protuberance by centuries of mutation, seemed strange; and I knew my green eyes glowed in the dark. Yes, I was wilder than any; I was the sorcerer, the land-walking belly-slitting father of the sharks.

We can easily forget, sometimes, that writers are like musicians or dancers. They train so intensively, they master so many technical elements, in order, in the long run, to break beyond all that technique into the pure rush of both real and, if lucky, original expression. But it's a strange paradox, isn't it, to think it has this combination of control and something beyond control.

—*John Lent*

Born in North Battleford, Catherine Buckaway was a prolific poet and playwright who published over two thousand poems as well as several plays. Catherine was one of North America's leading writers of Japanese miniature poetry forms.

THE SOURIS SINGS

Colour of sky
current breathes
the prairie

> *white-tailed deer*
> *elusive as elves*
> *leap from thickets*

buffalo tithed in blood
gnaw minutes
from the flutes of day

> *gentle hills*
> *wear green-fire*
> *gowns*

sundrops like rainbows
on parchment water

> *shadows shape*
> *the river's edge*
> *as day dims*

night breezes
brush the campfires
free from memories
seeded in the stars

> *the world*
> *changes*
> *to fold back*
> *unbidden Time*

Greg Button was born and raised in Moose Jaw, Saskatchewan, where he currently lives and writes.

IN MY DEFENCE

i pledge my allegiance sir
to the tree in my back yard

i swear to follow the laws
of alley cats and clouds

i vow that the grass
shall always tickle my feet

and i promise to be loyal
to little fat flies

especially the ones now buzzing
above your bald head sir

IN THE WHITE ROOM

their faces were walls
their lips
narrow as needles

i was strapped
to the trolley
they greased ready
the electrodes

i remember crying out
those moments
before the blackness

can recall now
their faces
clear and clean
cold as disinfectant

Anne Campbell was born and raised in Saskatchewan, and educated at the University of Regina. She has worked as a public relations officer in museums and art galleries, and most recently at the Regina Public Library. She has published several volumes of poetry since 1983.

MIGRAINE

The pain in my head
is a basket a donkey carries,   one
           that slips to the right on a climb,
        down a rock trail, one
   that disturbs
a left field of vision,   or the pain

        is heavy, a yolk,
        egg gone solid
       waiting to be born.

HEART EXCHANGE

Dying comes
not from the surgery

exchange heart to heart
but from rejection

a body
not able to accept
foreign matter   no experience

in letting   go
finding a mother's lap
to catch the fall.

ELVIS SETS IT FREE
for and with Tim and Mary

Elvis, Elvis, Elvis they cried
and I was a teenager when I saw him
above the waist   on TV

this protected us from his power
                    to loose sex.

Running now decades later to Elvis playing
ALL SHOOK UP, my tight spine, the small of my back
all shake free : his beat unlocks cells

and there have been sightings too, of this man
like a saint he comes,   apparition in the night.

He looses groins, that's his touch. He sets them free

the other night talking theology,
we spoke of *theandric*, Tim said it's called, the impulse
to call forth in love, in one deep gaze,
a single blade of grass, a man, the truth in each creation.

He looses groins, Elvis does
for God; he repeats it and repeats it
like a saint, he makes that miracle.

ORANGES

Hot, I remember the heat of the day
        stopped in time
        climbing a steep hill
     in one of the old black cars

       then we are parked
          in dust and silence
    in the middle of a prairie town
     in front of a hotel door

I am five years old
      and though they are there
   I don't see my sisters   in this memory
               only I   am standing
                    by the car
                door
                watching

     then he is there
   my dad
      and we buy oranges   an offering
             for my grandmother
           waiting
       in fast growing dark   and the point
      the point of this poem:

      I am five, for godsake
my grandmother meets us, her lamp turned low
   my father hands her oranges, and I know
        all of this
      offering is wrong

Poetry is the rhythm of our sex.

— Dave Margoshes

Ken Cathers was born and lives in Ladysmith on Vancouver Island. He has degrees from the University of Victoria and from York University. Since 1976, he has published several books of poetry. He works in a pulp mill in Nanaimo, B.C.

BLUE HERON

thin boned thing
from the grey world
I grew out of

poised
in some dark
part of me

the sight of it
wheeling in atop
shore cedar

perched on the
sky. etched
image   remembered

from the first
shrill call   echoing
across these waters.

AS I WRITE THIS DOWN

times he came home
on the short haul
stand out

had to show us
something he was
good at

way his face set
turning into the pit
away from us

pulling the wheel round
slow   hand over hand
his arms thick

in a shirt   sweat
stained   stinking of
sun   hot tar

(that was him)

other times he
snapped out of it
hated me
for baseball   striking
out   every game   cursed me
in the car   finally

after the season   for
not making him proud
drove home

sullen   & died the next morning
nothing more said
between us

left a silence
my sons have
to live with

this door closed
between us
as I write this down

REWRITE

hard to believe
I wrote
any of this

not recognizing
the images, lines
running on

past all breaks
of breath, pause
no sense

to the transitions
of phrase. there is
only one explanation

I have changed
 completely   between
the writing & revision

cannot even guess
at what it was
 once like
            to be me.

ICARUS

strange weather here
            believe me

when I say
odd showers
I mean frogs
cuttlefish

sometimes incredible
black larvae
pelting down
from a clear sky

I'm beginning
to think
            something's wrong here

have given up
explaining
small miracles

rats in the toilet
snakes in the tap

just pieces
that don't fit
this world
I thought
            I lived in

go ahead
name a reason

meteorites, geysers,
atmospheric inversion

it doesn't matter
anything is possible

this poem
could keep writing
into a lost
language

become
an animal
snuggling
in your hand

don't look up
waiting

by the time
you read this
everything could be
changed

a man
may have fallen
out of the sky
unnoticed

Marilyn Cay was born in Prince Albert, Saskatchewan. She presently lives with her husband on a mixed farm near Tisdale, Saskatchewan. She devotes as much time to her poetry as farm life will allow.

BLUE

words collect
blue robin eggs in my nest heart
all winter
incubating
I find them in the garden
in May
near the apple tree
empty halves
gaping at the sky

IN THE POCKET OF HER SON'S JEANS

a woman's headache
is in the pocket of her son's jeans
along with other minor interruptions
in his life
a warning from the cops, his report card
the bill for fixing his stereo
some change and his lighter
things, far from his centre, where he is king
and god almighty
he dumps it all on his dresser

at 2 a.m., kicks the jeans in the corner
they need washing
he sleeps
long and lean
his mouth open

PRIDE

he challenges his father
to arm wrestle
and the two ready themselves
at the kitchen table
this time
there is something about the son's calmness
that makes the father insist upon a fair start
his arm tense
the father breaks with speed
in order to put his son's arm down soundly

but he meets with iron this time
the two arms tremble, straight up and down
muscles bulging
hands gripping tightly

afterwards the mother says
the father was the big winner
even though it is her son
whose strength prevailed

TO DAUGHTER

it's cliché but
your eyes really are like cornflowers
so blue and round
your smile angelic
I don't know why you resisted my mothering
never fit
my opinions

I crumpled your ideas
like papers, now
that you're gone
I dig them out of the waste can
cast them across my table
finger them
and think they are valid

SEEDING TIME

I dream our combine see it coming
big and self-propelled across a field
swallowing a forgotten swath from last fall
fast coming so fast it begins to buck
the pick-up reaching into the sky then
catching dirt on its way down nearing
the hedge it doesn't slow or stop or veer
                    it punches
                  a hole
          through five rows of trees
lurches through the yard my husband slumped at the wheel

the combine finally stops far out in another field
the one he's hell-bent to finish seeding if it kills him

NO TIME FOR MICE

Robert Burns had time for mice
but I don't
the banker's leather shoe taps in town
I see the mice scamper on the combine's pick-up
wafted on the swath, racing
for the suicide edge
but the beast I ride is hungry and swift
and not paid for
we swallow them whole
and race on

HOME TOWN BOY

he is dressed casually
his shoes are smooth, tan, thin-soled
too fine for a small town in Saskatchewan
the folks know he must have bought them in Ottawa
maybe even Europe

the old café is gone and coffee row
is in the service station at the edge of town
the waitress flutters, doesn't know
what side to put his cup on
finally plops it down defiantly

he would like to sit with Charley
went to school with Charley
Charley was always the top dog

some of them saw the home town boy
at the banquet last night
chatting with the big shots at the head table
they point him out to each other on coffee row
it's been twenty years

yeah, I went to school with him
Charley nods in his direction
but doesn't look up
    hey
anybody know the price of flax this mornin'?

the home town boy busies himself
by soaking up the coffee in his saucer
with a napkin
his fine shoes under the table

What poetry can do is restore life, let language lead us to any number of promised lands, encourage it to flourish beyond its merely instrumental uses. What poets can do is listen, be humble, let language be.

— Gerald Hill

Lesley Choyce was born in New Jersey but moved to Nova Scotia in 1978 and became a Canadian citizen. He was educated at Rutgers University, Montclair State College and City University of New York. He teaches part-time at Dalhousie University, founded and runs Pottersfield Press and has written over 40 books of poetry, fiction and non-fiction. He lives on the seacoast near Halifax.

MY DOG WATCHES ME WRITE A POEM

She thinks it is a disease
and lends sympathy with her ears.
She has never trusted poems at all
and thinks them alive.
Right now, something has grabbed my hand
and causes a palsy
that blotches a clean page.

Curled up on the chair
like a completed stanza
the dog cannot endure the inhuman labour.
Her ears wait for the sound I make
at moments like this —
a high-pitched noise beyond human hearing.
The dog understands better
a world of immediacy.
When she tries to turn
experience into verse
it takes her whole body
to explode into loud imagery
that needs no footnotes.

ON BECOMING A CANADIAN CITIZEN

This month I became Canadian,
giving up on the tired, malignant love of America,
wanting the cold of a purifying north.
It's good to become a foreigner,
to pretend you are no longer what you were.
I'm giving up the arms race, the space race,
a chance to be a marine, an astronaut,
a President, a teller in the Chase Manhattan Bank,
a would-be assassin.

Physical changes will take place;
bones will grow back in hollow places
and my blood will turn a new colour.
The judge will ask my name and I will answer
Tundra, then sing anthems of geese,
track ice around the courthouse
and howl with my new-found Borealis.
All my friends will be there
helping me invent my new country
and sending postcards to the failed refugees south.

Someone will make me promise
to love an empire
stretched thin against an empty sky
but later, alone,
on a quiet hill,
the sea will question my politics,
the spruce will want more than professed loyalty
and the armies of the paranoid
will be short one soldier.

Peter Christensen grew up on a farm near Dickson, Alberta. He was educated at the University of Lethbridge. Peter has been publishing books of poetry since 1977. He has worked as a guide and Parks official in the Rocky Mountains. He lives and writes near Radium Hot Springs.

MOUNTAIN RESCUE

And so we fly, valkyries
in search of lost heroes.
Umbilically connected
by twelve meters of rope
taut to the belly of the war horse
Bell Jet Ranger helicopter
under whose whining blade
we hang, trust technocracy
to lower
my partner, stretcher and I
to the patient
whose stolid countenance
conveys the hard fate
of fallen mountaineers.

CHINOOK

in waves
down the mountains
to lift the white skirts
of old mother prairie.
Brings visions of summer
on the wind
smell of forests.

TRANSFORMATION

The last moment of sky
is a grey dusty rose.
Autumn rolls into place
colour wheels stop.

PRETENDING TO DANCE

I never feel I'm really dancing
when I'm dragged out on the floor.

I'm watching to see
if anybody is watching to see
if I'm watching them.

Why am I out here
shaking my limbs
doing some death shake
inside this cave?

THE OIL RUSH HAS COME

Broken bush and spruce
have roads
One room schools have gone
the way of the outhouse

All the little Europes have disappeared

In ten years
we have come   from wood   heat   shacks
to pink palaces

The back country is cutlined
marked square
drilled   pipelined
and torches burn

The plains are alive
with the campfires of millionaires

HAILSTORM

I remember the hailstorm
of 1952
as if I were a man then
My memory thickens
with each story
my father tells
of those hard years

I see him standing
in a ripened barley field
adrift in his garden

of winds and clouds
and grain
all ready for harvest

The sky goes grey and black
The barley heads begin
to sway their beards
caught in a desperate wind

Then there is a silence in the land
It smells of false truce
and my father's figure
transforms from farmer
to scarecrow
White stones
come running towards him
hail prancing
like horses' hooves
beating the yellow-kernelled stalks
flatly to the ground

I watched his heart
follow the hailstones
to the rich black earth
where side by side
lies the naked seed
and the melting winter

WASTED DOLLS

I asked you if you wanted
to shoot holes in the sky
kill a few tin cans
So we drive to the town dump
a few miles out
We take our rifles

from the gun rack above the seat
and bullet the magazines
I set bottles and cans
at a distance
and we count the broken
glass like trophies —
the shots echo for miles
with loudness
in the river valley below

The gun barrels are warm
our hands restless
and we scrounge through the junk
for new targets
I find a doll from a childhood
a doll thrown here
after age made it meaningless
We handle the doll
back and forth like glass
and our eyes begin
to dare each other
I set the doll against
a bullet-scarred car
pace back fifty yards
flip a coin
the doll's chest explodes —
our shots echo
as sawdust drains to the ground

The guns have emptied the doll
Smiles cut our faces
and we laugh not knowing
if we should feel guilty
or crazy
We fire our last bullets
at the sky like madmen —

the echo brings our laughter
and the guns roar back at us
There is silence and rubble
all around us
We walk to the truck
and put our tools away

Sometime later in our lives
I come to visit
and you have a baby daughter
and in the long afternoon
I ask you if you want to go
shoot a few tin cans
But you refuse
are busy tending the new life
you have created
You hand me the talc
as if it will shock my fist
fill the space
that craves the palm of my hand
There is a new loudness
to fill your hours
A new echo that you cannot ignore

HOME COMING

When I go home
I will face my oldest friends
Like the seeds left
from last year's harvest
they have fallen to the same fields
their fathers sowed
They are volunteer grain
They are the sons of farmers
a son like me

only I was one of those who
moved away to work
moved up north
moved to the city   got educated
moved finally into the mountains

It is fall and
they will be busy
roaring around the fields like woodbees
busy turning the soil
busy farming
They will ask me
why I did not stay
We will eat a farm meal
and talk about the good life
in the country
Talk about the millions
who starve
Talk about hail and fertilizer
and their fathers will ask me
about the world out there
as they slide back
into their armchairs
and appraise their strong sons

*When the poet is finished with the poem, it has become something else
sprouting a life of its own. It's a lively cycle, this creative cycle, which is
why it can be so unclear, so complex, so joyful.*

— *Lorne Daniel*

John Livingstone Clark was born on Saltspring Island, British Columbia. He is a graduate of the University of British Columbia. John teaches English at St. Peter's College, Muenster and the University of Saskatchewan. Since 1990 he has published five books of poetry. He lives in Dundurn, just out of Saskatoon.

EXISTENTIAL BREAKFAST

It isn't clear how I faced-off with mortality while
eating breakfast at the Broadway Café, but I did, staring
hungrily down at my poached eggs, bacon and hashbrowns.
I started thinking up a story: in it, a very old man is
asked about the key to longevity. His response? "Grease!
A good greasy plate of grub every morning — then a smoke
over the local newsrag." It seemed funny at the time,
trowelling jam on the well buttered toast, but as I de-
molished my coronary special, I could see I was gorging
in bad faith — just whistling past the urn. I'd never
see sixty, not with my lust for hot grilled ambrosia —
cholesterol was building a Great Wall around my heart,
loyalty to working class tucker like a tombstone around
my neck — without sprouts I was doomed. When the end
comes, I mused, I'll be seated at this table inhaling
fried spuds, dripping eggs and glazed ham — hashslingers
will bear my carcass on a teacart, the chef weeping at the
waste, at the ragout I might have graced.

Grief stricken and terrified I could barely stand to pay
my bill. I'm sorry, I whimpered, I don't have change for

a tip. But the waitress smiled like an angel, and just
squeezed my trembling hands — Don't worry, she said, it's
a pleasure to serve you. And there shone heaven through
pearly white teeth: a full refund guaranteed or a bromide
on the house.

GAVIN'S FEET: THE PERILS OF NEGATIVE THEOLOGY

Gavin comes down the blue wooden stairs
with old black sweat pants rolled up
to reveal his calves. Slowly, with a thump,
his small bare feet hit the steps. Slowly
the pale translucent flesh of his legs
descends before my eyes — as I sit
in the basement at my desk, pulling my
beard and dreaming of God.

God is everywhere and nowhere, someone
once said. If so, how can he remember
all the names of the damned? How
can he notice every feather of every
skylark eaten by every cat? I
feel comfortable in this knowledge, that
God is everywhere and nowhere. At least
half the time I'm in the clear.

Chris Collins was born in Ottawa, Ontario. He grew up in Saskatoon and graduated from the University of Saskatchewan. He is now teaching English in Chunchon, Korea.

MARKS

think of
the marks on this page
as wild
pawprints in snow

I make no promises
of destination
within their loops
only
that something intangible
was here
now
(or is it
already then?)
and has
for an instant
clawed
struggled
and dissolved
all before you blink

DUCK HUNTING

we hate one another
and before dawn drive over thirty miles
to this isolated field
crouch a hundred yards apart
to shoot over each other's head

feeling as father and son

we sight lines into the grey
fire to clear the air
of bats
between the blinded positions

dropping them without a thought

UTOPIA MUST BE HERE — SO WHERE ARE THE JOBS?

Utopia must be here
since our postman asks
"any trouble with the French Surrealists?"
while handing over bills and coupons

a busdriver with Junior Mints and Thucydides
on the dash
Debussy in a Walkman

and at Safeway a boy bag groceries
while quoting a Stoic philosopher
"adapt yourself to the environment in which
your lot has been cast and show true love
to the fellow mortals with whom
destiny has surrounded you"

with that voice's profile, Marcus Aurelius
tattooed on a forearm flying over broccoli
two thousand years dead and orating above my Oreos
competing with the beep and computer-monotone
of the talking register

"Utopia must be here," I remark at Ultracuts
and she responds, blowdrying with a degree in Sociology
"Oh, let's do a study. Trim the sideburns?"

KID SKY

It's a dot the spot in your life
you start the change
from a slow, sloth-like
but sure state of dream
to deal in flashing figures
theories and ideas
that, to see
needs be to stare
and burrow with your mind
until a sky-whole view of things
is almost lost
to a pinhole star of light

become delight
to see that kid
stepping, dare-devil style
along the rail-line and looking
between its ties
for agates, Indian hammerheads

anything of interest and
watch him stop
before he sees me looking
to gaze at a moon
in the heat and prairie-blue sky
of this, his summer

Like a tiny mammal amid dinosaurs, poetry looks very weak when compared with money, provides more pleasures than money can, and will outlast money.

— Tom Wayman

Dennis Cooley was born in Estevan, Saskatchewan and obtained degrees from the University of Saskatchewan and the University of Rochester. He is a professor of English at St. John's College, University of Manitoba. He is a poet, anthologist, literary critic and editor.

YOU TAKE MY LOVE

                                      like a dog
          you lope off
      with it
           my love
              a chewed T-bone
        in yr jaw
           & you looking back
              over yr shldr
                    as if you might be caught

              & now I find my
    self wondering
             : what if
      you took it
    & you bury it
        /somewhere/
          & forget where
    it is

Writers invent words and new uses for words because words are the tools they use every day.

                              —*Jim Green*

Lorna Crozier was born in Swift Current, Saskatchewan. She attended the Universities of Saskatchewan, Regina and Alberta. She is currently teaching in the Writing Department at the University of Victoria. Her collection *Inventing the Hawk* won the Governor-General's Award for poetry in 1992. She is regarded as one of Canada's leading poets.

TRAINS

As a boy
he pressed his ear to the rail
and heard the hum of distant trains;
he balanced on the polished line
arms outstretched like a Clyde Beatty acrobat,
and paced his step to the measure of the ties.
Under the trestle he had his first orgasm
his rush pounding to the beating of the wheels.

What better way to die —
to meet the train's roar
around the coulee's bend
to flatten
like a child's penny
warm on steel.

She bricked the eastern windows,
the ones that faced the track.
In the morning the house
was cold and dark.

She never saw a sunrise
or a train again
but twice a day
the cups shook in their saucers
and her breastbone thundered.

JEWISH CEMETERY AT LIPTON

They built a village
for their dead
body-long houses of brick or wood
metal grain-bin roofs
headstones crusted with lichen rough
on smooth stone on smooth fingers
marble meant for reading
cut with Hebrew letters
        Moses Raichman
        Grandma Schwartz
or wooden markers
the letters slivered by wind and rain

They planted no trees
but sage   wolf willow   buffalo beans
push through the fence   the mortar,
a star of David rises over grass heads
bent with yellow seeds

In the coffin shed a swallow nest,
a pot-bellied stove for winter warmth

We walk between the prairied dead
touching stone touching wood touching hands
Build for me a wooden house
with one open window

INNER SPACE

my spaces are vast
           are blue

winds rip through my ribcage

redtails shriek in my throat

with a dry puckered mouth
the sun sucks my brain

i look small
and earthbound

           but inside/

is   the   sky

Michael Cullen was born in Lethbridge, Alberta. He is a graduate of Mount Royal College, Calgary, and the University of Western Ontario. He writes for the screen, for theatre, and reviews books and plays for a Vancouver Island newspaper. He teaches at the University of Victoria and lives in Sidney, B.C.

SOUTH OF FORT MACLEOD AT A BUFFALO JUMP

here the chase ended
the buffalo were rounded and pushed
where they
jumped
frightened   a ton and a half
falling
down
down
the cliffs of the buffalo jump
where the hunt ended
where the prairie ends
finds the gully   the sandstone cliff
the napi-tahta river cutting
deeper
and deeper
into the prairie tundra

no glacier warped this
the buffalo fell
foaming at the mouth
gasping through black nostrils
the nonsense of the senses
warped
not knowing right from left

down from up
blindly running into a frenzy
blind
kicking dust as air
where earth was prairie
expanse
abrupt
a ton and a half
neck muscles tightening
the hump bracing
for whatever fall
to end

hunters at the bottom
waiting to slit with bone knife
those who land
and in brayed defiance
attempt to stand

Once I saw a fossilized imprint of a hand in a museum of natural history. That simple sight — a wave from a long-ago actual human hand — struck me. I felt the essence of what poetry is at that moment, being both startled and struck with a sudden sense of knowing.

— *Marilyn Cay*

Lorne Daniel was born in Edmonton, Alberta, and educated at the Universities of Lethbridge and Calgary. He lives in Red Deer, Alberta.

IN THE FOLD

living below ground level, in love
we hauled laundry in green garbage bags
to the laundromat six blocks away
folded white sheets together
one at each end
our lips meeting as we drew the ends
together

with the kids here and me working
away, you took to folding alone
in the basement of our rented house
holding the middle in your teeth
while each arm pulled a corner to the centre
this was the way your mother did it you said

last year you no longer saw the need
for folding
instead taking sheets direct from the dryer
to the bed
they always wrinkle anyway and we had
a bigger bed now, in the house we built, besides
the machines downstairs were so handy
it only made sense

today as I try to teach the kids
to work together folding our single sheets

they ask why I can't do it alone
and I have nothing
to keep them interested
                    in the fold
say nothing, turning away
from thoughts of your phone call
yesterday from a laundromat

THE FALLS

As we climb further from the trailhead
the rivers jump
narrow and swift
through young rock cuts
and I pause at the wreckage of a foot bridge
                    broken and brushed aside
while the children scramble over the timbers
bubbling with adventure, testing agilities
learned on balance beams and karate mats

It will be our only holiday of the year
and as the riversound winds down behind us
we weave through cool spruce forest
with an easy scuffle and growing quiet
broken now and again
by brief clear bursts, approaching falls

Kate and Eric chase the sound, call after the playful mist
until they dash free onto the falls' rock shelf
drawn to the water's rushing edge
as I call out, river's roar pushing the words
back down my nervous throat
Call out again, warning, warning
looking at the spray's light mist

on time smoothed rocks and the delicate prints
the children's gym shoes leave

And it just takes that moment, a slip,
and there is no time to stop Kate
catapulting, doing a cartwheel/back spring
over the brink, Eric
throwing a side-kick into the mist
and tumbling, forearm up in classic defence
I see them splash into the quick green
throw up arms of water
dancing from stone to stone
See them disappear and reappear over and over again
bounce off boils of stone and plunge into the current
see them bob up, riverfoam in their mouths

When they are spent and the river releases them
again to me I will take them up
gather them in the dark and quiet embrace
of pine where they will rest
And as they lie
still, finally, I will close
these startled eyes

BONE DANCE

she is not a phenomenon
she is not a magazine story in black and white
with photos before and after

she has just gone home
leaving our faces drawn and thin
it is a clear morning
and she has had a shock
'a shock through my brain'

one day, she said, she ate
a muffin and drank a glass of water

most days she won't say

shopping always for smaller sizes
smaller now than at twelve years
spinning, today, to show us the swirl
a new skirt
she is happy with

for an instant she is lost in colour
but stops, white

dizzy, spinning still
she is dizzy more morinings than not
she has always been called dizzy, she says
but she has not always agreed so

she is 82 pounds and counting
down
moving in on her self, hard
as she can be: no excess
no other, no wrong, only

the white of bone, the pure
choreography, elemental

her dance free of flesh

H.C. Dillow was born in New York City. He was educated at the City College of New York and the University of London. He taught English at Adelphi College on Long Island and at the University of Regina. He lives in Regina, Saskatchewan.

WINTER MOUSE

Twenty below it was
When we found him in the garage,
In the old bin where we keep the grain we scatter to birds
On winter mornings,
Skittering round over the shifting surface
Like young thoughts in an old man's brain,
Replete to a roundness
But leaping desperately for the bin's edge
A good six inches above his head,
Eye-buttons dark with fear,
Stretching on feet delicate as ice ferns
On a frosted pane.

Our four gloved hands to reach him out,
Cold, and afraid of squeezing too hard,
Amazed at the quickness
Of the small life under the fur,
At the string tail
And the gloriously extravagant ears.

Then, abruptly still, curled for a moment
In a leather palm —
Up, over the edge,
And down, scuttling into shadows,
Barely touching the frozen earth of the floor.

Hands numb with cold
We fumbled with books and car keys
As we'd fumbled with that living quicksilver
In the bin a moment before,
And questioned the morning light
For tokens of a thaw —
Having learned the value of such minor portents
When mice and lovers bide a precarious season
Sharing a cold edge for balance —
For signs that this day at least
Might keep some measure in its rougher weather,
And keep our lives together.

MOLE

Under the root he plies,
Despoiled of his share of grace:
Spirit without eyes,
Body with wrinkled face.

The seasons go and come;
All times to him are dark.
The digging is still the sum,
The progress, and the mark.

Thin hands revert to hooks
Beneath the stony sod,
Refusing to question books
Or grasp at proofs of God.

Whether the beast can pray
Or comprehend the light,
He cannot see by day
And does not err by night.

The best of poetry is a kind of breathing, a sighing of sound that creates both satisfaction and meaning beyond itself as it falls in rhythms already existing in the bodies of both writer and reader.

— *Anne Campbell*

Paulette Dubé is an Albertan who has written and published poetry in both English and French. She is a graduate of the Faculté St. Jean of the University of Alberta. She has published several books of poetry and teaches school in Jasper where she lives.

PAUSE DURING A WINTER SKY

surrounded by laundry
making pea soup
tendrils of ham fat cooking
kiss her ears and face

the wood shifts a note
sighing within the stove
the house weighs heavy
she knows

the wooden spoon
to sway the peas
wave an onion piece
away to one side
then another

she feels the ticking of the clock
as the dance of her own heart
pulling time, discarding seconds
healing, smoothing the fat bubble
out of the soup
into the bowls

at the window through the mirror
coloured balls of children tumble closer

L'ORAGE

I smell oranges on my hands
the air around me hums
a door slams under the hand of the West One

turn to see
frenzied cat's paw zipping the lake
a wet ripple of white grey
the trees groaning
turning a pale palm up

the curls shift a note
see the house warmth whirl out
hear the static smell of singed hair

I read dead flies in the sill dust
entrails for modern wizards
twitches of lightning
snipslashing through pregnant air
I breathe deep at the thunder

turn my skin inside out
and drink the storm

THE TREES DANCE BARE

it's dry time
when the wind comes flitting
and fighting from the hills
the heaving and the sighs

bold colours fold up and go south
the trees hear and dance bare

littered leaves make their escape
whirling the air with mute mouths

all things wild and forgotten
all things tossed and rotten
take centre stage
for a reason

A WOMAN IN A PORTRAIT OF LACE

i have my demons
who won't let me sleep

i have my angels
my soul to keep

i dream my heaven
i live my hell
i have big sounds
of tolling bells

not the spry wee one
i used to be
Mother Nature ate the better of me

Poetry is the rhythm of language, which is the medium not only of our speech but of our dreams, our wishes.

— Dave Margoshes

Leona Gom was born on a farm near Hines Creek, Alberta, and lived there for twenty years. She graduated from the University of Alberta, and has gone on to hold several teaching positions. She has published both poetry and fiction and lives in White Rock, B.C.

MOVED

The earth begins, already,
to reclaim what once was trees;
rotting logs collapse,
roofs are bending
in a slow ballet,
and everywhere
the green grass fires
lick at lumber.
Already sold, these acres
will be ploughed next year,
remains of buildings
burned or buried,
and a field of grain,
hungry for the newly-broken soil,
will rise from the forgotten
bones of barns.
Around the yard
the farm machines,
strangely still this fall,
grow from rubber, tired stems.
Their metal blossoms,
huge and red and rusty,

await their own harvest —
auction.
    And we three — born here,
who grew here,
who climbed the trees
    ran down the river-banks,
    swam in the dugout,
    hid in the hayloft,
    rode horses as rein-free as we —
grown weary of wonder now,
cling to our separate cities,
refusing to repay this farm
for what it was
and what we are.

WIDOW

    The clothes were the hardest to face,
the most personal.
She asked the children, urgently,
if they wanted them.
"No," they said, misjudging her need,
and repelled by the thought
of wearing his clothes
or disposing of them.
    They hung in the closet for months,
the shirts pressing against her dresses,
the pants beside them on the hangers
with a thin tumour of dust.
She would see them every night
as she undressed,
and every morning they were
the first thing she saw,
hanging there, waiting,

each item speaking dumbly to her
of when it was bought
and where it was worn
and why it is worn no more.
And she would turn her head away,
to the cold mate of her pillow,
and weep with that terrible anguish of loss.
	But still she could not bear
to take them down.
	When the children came home,
they saw them there,
but they could not speak of it to her.
They thought of the day
they would be taking down her clothes,
piling his and hers together,
as perhaps it should be.

SURVIVAL

There was never gentleness.
All this romantic bullshit
about growing up on farms.
All I remember
are the pain and death.
When pigs were castrated,
their screams all afternoon
and my father coming in,
the guilty blood all over him.
When calves were dehorned,
their desperate bawling
and my mother saying,
"it doesn't really hurt them."
When I saw kittens smashed
against the barn walls,

and dogs shot
when they were too old
to herd the cattle,
and chickens
with their severed heads
throbbing on the bleeding ground,
and horses shipped
when my father bought a tractor,
and I could bus to school.
I learned a lot about necessity,
that things are functional, or die;
and I was not as ill-equipped
as first I thought
to live in cities.

METAMORPHOSIS

Something is happening
to this girl.

She stands on one leg
on the third block
of her hopscotch game,
lifts herself forward
to the next double squares,
and, as she jumps,
something changes.

Her straight child's body
curls slowly in the air,
the legs that assert themselves
apart on the squares
curve in calf and thigh,
angles become arches;
her arms pumping slowly

to her sides adjust
to a new centre of gravity,
the beginnings of breasts
push at her sweater,
her braids have come undone
and her hair flies loose around her.

Behind her
the schoolhouse blurs,
becomes insubstantial
and meaningless,
and the boys in the playground
move toward her,
something sure and sinister
in their languid circling.

Slowly she picks up the beanbag.
When she straightens,
her face gathers
the bewildered awareness
of the body's betrayal,
the unfamiliar feel
of the child's toy
in her woman's hand.

BLIZZARDS

It was
    he said
the horizontal snow
that drove her mad
    blowing in thin and endless chains
    across our windows

not pulling itself down
into the reason of the right angle
    but that constant tearing across
eroding the expectation of gravity
    the vertical reassurance
    on the flat landscape

There was only
that white streaming
into the corners of her eyes
across the pointless prairie

THE WAY HE TOLD IT

Such cold,
the horses white with it,
and my wife, dying,
in the sleigh,
forty miles to hospital,
then getting there,
and they wouldn't take her in.
No money, no doctor,
they said.
And Rosenbloom, he was there,
you take this woman in, he yelled,
I'll pay your goddamned money!
So then it was all right,
they would take her in.
He was a Jew, Rosenbloom, they said,
but this is what I remember of him.

THESE POEMS

These poems are homesick.
They keep crawling out
      from under my pen
and running back
      to the north.
They will not be domesticated.
They will not be toilet-trained.
They mess all over the page
with their persistent images
      of farm,
they chew through their ropes
      of urban metaphors
and sneak away whenever they can.
And when there is no way out
they curl up spitefully
      underneath their titles
and starve themselves
      to death.

*Poems are stories we tell ourselves, often for reasons we can't explain.
Our need for stories is so fundamental that we make up our own stories,
even while we sleep.*

— Colin Morton

Jim Green is a poet, raconteur, writer, broadcaster and performer.
He spent his early years in the lee of the Rocky Mountains. For
the past 30 years he's lived and worked in Fort Smith in the North
West Territories.

DEAD HORSE WINTER

He made it back to the ranch
in two long days snow piled
three feet when he left town,
covered the top wires
by dawn next morning
as he leap-frogged along
with two worn-out horses
lunging at chest deep drifts.

The cattle were bawling
bunched up in the creek bed.
He sucked them out with the smell
of loose hay and a trail
punched through by Clydesdales
dragging the sled. He set out
next day for the horses
but his mounts bogged down
just short of the ridge.
He jammed his saddle in a tree
sent the horses on the backtrail
and floundered on alone
with snowshoes made of aspen,
strips from a grey blanket
and strings from the saddle.

The last days were the worst,
searching the still canyons
for stranded   wasted bands,
the killing   blood
splattered dark on crystal white,
the numbing slam of the rifle
and the screams.
The lucky ones were dead
already   the rest were almost gone,
slumped walleyed in soft snow
just slack hide and hard bones,
they had no tails left and
even manes were missing where
they'd chewed on each other.
Sticks poked through
slashed cheeks   gums raw
bloodied from crushing branches,
the last of the feed.
He shot and kept shooting,
killed a hundred and more
first with a long gun
till he ran out of shells,
finished the last of them off
with an old Savage shotgun.

In the spring   a gelding
with eight gaunt mares in tow
came down from the valley.

DRUM SONG

bum bum bum bum bum bum bum bum bum bum bum
bum bum bum bum bum bum bum bum bum bum bum
bum bum bum bum bum bum bum bum bum bum bum
bum bum bum bum bum bum bum bum bum bum bum

The drums   the drums   the beat of the drums
the beat of the drums   the beat of the heart
the beat of the heart   the throb of the land
the throb of the land   the throb of life
the throb of life in the beat of the drums
the power   the power   the beat of the drums
the drums   the heart   the land   the life
the power in the heart of the drums of life
the drums   the drums   the beat of the drums

I'm sitting on dried grass facing the water
bum bum bum bum bum bum bum bum bum bum bum
the sun is sinking behind the black islands
bum bum bum bum bum bum bum bum bum bum bum
a raven stiff wings by to its nightly roost
bum bum bum bum bum bum bum bum bum bum bum
an end of the day loon call rings clear
bum bum bum bum bum bum bum bum bum bum bum
Women soft step the log dock with tin pails
bum bum bum bum bum bum bum bum bum bum bum
bend to crack the skim ice with their heels
bum bum bum bum bum bum bum bum bum bum bum
scoop up cold water for empty tea kettles
bum bum bum bum bum bum bum bum bum bum bum
and a kid runs by pushing a small red wagon
bum bum bum bum bum bum bum bum bum bum bum
a load of water in a green plastic barrel
bum bum bum bum bum bum bum bum bum bum bum

Behind me   the throb   the beat of the drums
the beat of the drums   the throb of life
the throb of the drums   the beat of death
the beat   of death

bum bum bum bum bum bum bum bum bum bum bum
bum bum bum bum bum bum bum bum bum bum bum

bum bum bum bum bum bum bum bum bum bum bum
bum bum bum bum bum bum bum bum bum bum bum

The old lady knew she was going to die
had them fly her back to the settlement
beside the clear lake where she was born
Word was sent out to the other villages
people arrived by boat   plane   and canoe

They came   shook her hand   said farewell
to the tired grey lady of ninety years
grandmother to half the town
come home to die

She smiled to see her friends once more
listen to the waves slap the sand shore
the sharp fall wind in the swaying pine

She died Wednesday
everyone gathered at the small log house
clasping her still hand   a final touch
drinking tea and quietly playing checkers
Planes came Thursday and more the next day

The burial by the lake was Friday
with preparations for the feast underway
they burned her clothes on the beach
a blaze of dry willows on the sand

Hung her thin mocassins in a tall pine
sung hymns in the wind-blown cemetery
cooking pots   bubbling in every house

In the evening the people came together
the visitors   relatives   and the kids
carrying pots   buckets   and tea kettles
The young men served for the feast
kept serving till there was no more
plates piled high with fresh roast caribou

steaming white fish   trout   warm bannock
apples   oranges   jam   butter   lard
a bowl of blood soup   canned peaches
and gallon after gallon of tea
Almost an hour to share all the food
enough to last everyone there for days

Then came the speeches
old men remembering yesterday
talking about today   about death
about the land   about life   about tomorrow
After the feast   the drums   the dancing
together   round and round the log hall
the swaying circles pulsing to the drums
through the night   into the morning

That was yesterday   today
the drums are going strong again
as I sit near the still lake shore
only there is a difference today
The drums speak another language
as the skins are heated for the hand game
a hand game   a game of power
a game of power   a game of life

a gambling game   a game of money
a game of skill   a game of power
a game of the drum   a game of life

Getting up from the brittle grass
I walk down to the drum house
where the teams have been picked
the drum skins warmed up
and the chants are rising
the game has begun
I step into the drum thunder

It is a new beat   a sound of the heart
the beat of the heart   the sound of life
the throb of life in the beat of the drums
the power in the heart of the drums of life
the drums   the drums   the beat of the drums
the beat   of life

kaBUM kaBUM kaBUM kaBUM kaBUM kaBUM kaBUM
kaBUM kaBUM kaBUM kaBUM kaBUM kaBUM kaBUM
kaBUM kaBUM kaBUM kaBUM kaBUM kaBUM kaBUM
kaBUM kaBUM kaBUM kaBUM kaBUM kaBUM kaBUM

The poet stands with his finger on the pulse of the world, and it is his dreams and visions that measure the health of the beating heart.

— Greg Button

Helen Hawley was born in Swift Current, Saskatchewan, and studied Fine Art at the Universities of Regina and Toronto, as well as at the Sorbonne in Paris. She has worked in various publishing houses in London, England where she lives. Her artwork has been exhibited in several countries.

WINDS OF MY COUNTRY

In my own country
the winds flood down the prairie
from the northwest,
bluewhite in winter, roar rumours of life
over the surging icefields.
Winds stream
clear in summer but carrying
scent of sage, increment of dust,
fanning the furrowed earth and the high beardgrass
not lasciviously; here one revels in sparseness,
hint of slough, pale flash of rose
under the Russian thistle.

Flesh draws breath, insistence rises
with every wind freshet,
with every morning's rising sun
till suddenly the heat is everywhere,
stinking of thaw; there are no springs here.
Oh river of winds from the northwest,
or night winds, sightless where I now stand,
turn me about
like a leaf in your currents,
shout me your courses
or overflow into the brimming eyes of the earth.

Patrick Lane

What we must come to is authority, a taking upon ourselves the rich voice that is in us and acknowledging it; to say what must be said in spite of ourselves, admit to what is both right and wrong in us and make of those choices a witness to the world. At the heart of authority is integrity. What we risk most is our own truth; it is of ourselves, "the foul rag and bone shop of the heart," as Yeats said, but also of the world. All our perceptions are images, each tree, each blade of grass, each bird, and every image we conjure out of ourselves becomes us and so represents our humanity. The stunted desert pines of my childhood in the desert country of the Okanagan are emblems of a higher order and carry with them all the resonance that resides in the words *desert*, *pine*, and *stunted*. By naming we affirm our world with all its griefs and miseries, its triumphs and joys. When I say, in the poem "Brother",

> *Sometimes when I'm afraid I walk into the hills*
> *where the trees are. Stunted desert pines*
> *the world leaves alive because they're useless.*
> *The earth is made of terrible stones and sand.*

then I am speaking of childhood with all its suffering and the *pines* become symbolic of the brothers in my poem, their birth and rising into manhood, "small, tough, because the days kept hurting us."

If there is authority in the poem I've just referred to then it arises out of a central truth about myself and is maintained by the tone contained in the particular words chosen. They are the frame of the mind, the inflected music that is the expression of feeling I wish to convey. All poems are a musical score for the voice. Each sound, each musical phrase, creates mood and so creates the feeling we are trying to elicit. Authority is probity, a strict honesty. Authority is a private voice we overhear. Where authority is found we find knowledge. Elizabeth Bishop spoke of saltwater, the deep

dark ocean which is ourselves, in her poem "At the Fishhouses".
She says,

> It is like what we imagine knowledge to be:
> dark, salt, clear, moving, utterly free,
> drawn from the cold, hard mouth
> of the world, derived from the rocky breasts
> forever, flowing and drawn, and since
> our knowledge is historical, flowing, and flown.

What is in the tone of her voice is what John Ashberry called,
in "And *Ut Pictura Poesis* Is Her Name?",

> The extreme austerity of an almost empty mind
> Colliding with the lush, Rousseau-like foliage of its desire to communi-
> cate
> Something between breaths, if only for the sake
> Of others and their desire to understand you and desert you

The voice of authority is the sound you hear inside the emp-
tiness of a great bell. In its immense silence is the sound of the
whole world waiting, expectant, and almost afraid, for the poem
to begin. But it is not simply in the great elegaic poems that we
find such authority and integrity of voice. The love lyric and the
small anecdotal lyric also resonate with authority. It is there just
as it is found in the brevity of the haiku, the sudden insight as if
dropped into the quiet pool of the mind. Here is one by the
Japanese poet, Basho, written in 1689,

> The beginning of all art:
> a song when planting a rice field
> In the country's inmost part.

John V. Hicks was born in London, England. As a child, he settled in Prince Albert, Saskatchewan, where he still resides. Hicks was awarded an Honourary Doctorate in Literature from the University of Saskatchewan, and he received the Saskatchewan Order of Merit. He has been writing and publishing poetry for over half a century.

THE LATE SUMMER WEEDS

Cool in the slant of sun, the garden
entertains here and there a late
visitor. Controls are done with,
days of toil diminish. These few
linger informal in the freshening
air, unthreatened, as after contentions
the playing field rests empty, loiterers
idling, cheering a fading echo.

Summer is threadbare. Even the light
is late. There were voices, and these
have dropped to a whisper of occasional
chirrups, part memory of nestings, part
projections into a long journey,
creative urgencies at rest,
acceptance of a season's ending,
gains forgotten, small losses untallied.

The heart too is still. Surges, strains,
pressings to victories, all softened now.
There is time for reflection, time
to refrain from determinations,

time to accept the sanctity
of silence, prepare in its depths
the entertainment of the new chilling
airs, the drawing in of darkness.

FELIX
A bishop's cat

Cats should curl
up. This one, on a whim,
rolls ungainly over,
spine swayed, legs and paws
extended, reaching out
as though to invite and embrace
something lingering just beyond
reasonable conjecture.

                    Felix,
by turns companion,
pacifist, killer,
what might these spirit speculations
be? Dare one inquire? We, smug,
from upper-end-of-scale assurance
look down with traces of
ill-advised derision.
A safer stance by far
to admit our sensual limitations,
to concede there are things it were wiser
never to question,
never to be known.

LITTLE MOUSE

Little mouse behind
my wainscot, be still
of your stirring.

It is Christmas Eve;
nativity is silence before
the first cry.

There are dusty stairs,
old attics, waiting
for silence to fall,

for starlight to shed
its blaze down
the quiet way.

Mouse in my wainscot,
you are gnawing a little hole
in my heart.

NATIVITY

They waited in the fields,
night and winter
throbbing at their ears,
eyes scanning the darkness
for prowling shapes
reflected in the firelight.

The tiding words
pierced the air like trumpets
sounding. How could they not

fulfil the quest, explore
that disturbance of history, the
upsetting of this quiet?

They insisted there were angels
singing hosannahs
that jewelled night, startling
the drowsing sheep.
       Peace and a sword
       dropped from the sky as one,
       shocked the simple shepherds
       fastfooting it to Bethlehem.

WIND IN THE CORN

Half way between my home and where I hastened
something within the misty autumn air
brought me up short, at once remembering
what I had meant to tell the odd-job man
whom I had left working the garden over,
raking it clean of old potato tops
and shrivelled pea vines with their sticks and strings,
smoothing the plot for winter's carpet-laying.
I dreaded lest I might be all too late,
even by speeding back the way I'd come,
and find him rooting up the withered corn.
For I had reckoned all the winter through
on hearing what the wind would have to say
to my two rows of parchment leaves and stalks
when no more audient foliage was about;
because in summer time this graceful folk
so busily employed within itself,
sucking the milk of the full-breasted earth,
laying white pearls along the cobs in rows,
and spinning silken tassels all night long,

89

must hardly heed the singing wind — less so
with fifty other songs opposing it.

But after harvest, even later on
when snow has spread a silence everywhere,
and beauty is withdrawn into the ground,
being touched by sleep, then the once comely leaves
are dry as death and ripe for talking to.
The wind says things in winter you'd not guess.
It was a good I did myself that day
for hurrying back and putting one to rights
about the wind and corn and what I wanted
that ever after stood me well in stead,
and in a final counting warded off
what would have set me back a full year's living
had it gone unaccomplished. I own friends
would do nigh anything for me for asking,
but none who'd leave two rows of dead corn grounded
on into winter for no better reason
than that I might drop by from time to time
and stand beside it when the wind was blowing.

DARK MORNING

Mother, there's a pterodactyl
perched on our aerial. He
bends it. When he folded his wings
he made the sun come out.

    Omens of extinction are
    everywhere. We don't need
    visitations of forgotten reptiles
    to twist our antennae awry.

You thought it was a dark morning.
It was his wing span, I tell you —

how many inches? No — pterodactyls
don't answer to inches.

Hand me that duster, will you?
Every day is a dark morning.

Here, mother. Let's not go extinct.
He's sitting there inventing feathers.

WINTER ZERO

To experience *nothing* you must see
the prairie town at mid-morning under its
stifle of snow. All the crops that ever were
are buried there, resting in peace. All the
hoppers that will ever be are down there
pinhead-eyed, unable to stroke crackling leg joints
yet, waiting for the swing of the world
to embrace the sun.
                                        Nothing
will warm itself barely over the night
fires, stamping feet and conversations
still putting fall to rest, still rolling
the dice of the next-year game, yellow windows
and thin smoke wreaths marking the banked fires
of hope, a belief in Coke signs on cafe sidings
blistering under the sun.
                                        Now
nothing has taken hold. One huddles
midway between past and future, arranges thoughts
in order, circulates opinion, learns to confront
this semblance of reality, the bitter cold.

SONNET FOR A SMALL GIRL

I cannot kiss you, frog, although you be
a prince in anatomic disarray,
although there may be truth in what you say,
and your release from spells waits only me
to strike the powers of darkness down and free
you from a witch's shackles, let the day
you hope for dawn, become the shining way
down which you'd ride. You have my sympathy,

dear frog, and yet I tell you I have heard
that love has necromancy of its own
to bring the heart to ruin. It is sad
to think the dream is much to be preferred
to waking, but how soon might you bemoan
your pond, the safety of your lily pad?

PAYOFF

I know what I'm doing;
I'll pass this one and pitch
to the blonde, ignoring
all your signals.
You want one that could provoke
a dribbling for the hole,
an easy play; side retired.
I want the blonde; right now,
not next time round. Frown
if you like, I'm
shaking you off. This is
my own affair. Relief?
No, the game's mine right through.

This one's a free ride.
Get ready — here comes
my wide breaker. Then
watch me get the blonde, like
in three straight throws.

SNAKE

A pity my earliest sight of you
wrote horror, loathing, revulsion on
the tablet of the mind, which letters are,
I fear, ineradicable. Fear
circled me, drew the noose tight,
made you metaphor. I cannot watch
your slithering ease, your perfect
symmetry, your silent essaying
of here to there, the miracle of
your curvic going (the angle unknown
to your fluid motion) without
dread seizing me, some agent of death
pointing a finger. In your innocence,
forgive me. The naturalist,
student of environment, beating
beneficial, beneficial, into my brain,
fails in his argument. My ears
are deaf, like yours.

TOWN SPRING

Indoors winter scenes
hang outdated.

Outdoors rotted snow
exposes rubbles of stones.

Dust takes the air
as trying its wings again.

Everything has aged
since leaves fell.

Is there a robin
somewhere?

Poetry fosters a passionate interest in language, its rhythm and emotional power. It inspires a willingness to write and revise until a poem is the closest you can get to what you want to say.

— Barbara Sapergia

Gerald Hill, born in Herbert, Saskatchewan, was educated at the University of Calgary and David Thompson University Centre, Nelson, B.C. He teaches at the University of Regina.

LABOUR DAY, UNEMPLOYED

Something is offensive
about a bureaucratic lizard
who sits so fat on a job opening
when you are looking for a job
(especially when you recognize this lizard
as one who emerged from your old high school
at the same time as your little sister).

Face to face across his desk
you think of the desert: mounds of shifting papers
paper clips that sting in the wind
and lizards sucking cactus flesh.
Then this lizard bursts
a brief curve in the sand; sand falls
from his back as he points
at your resume and speaks:

You've been there so far away?
Doing all these other things?
Why not remain still, in this heat
and rise in the normal manner upwards
towards the hot sky, the hot jobs
as I have done?

You gaze at him. He can stare back
forever without blinking

because he has the jobs
and you want one.

You know lizards don't have ears
but you tell him anyway of your experience
your qualifications for this position.

He only flicks his tail.
The interview is over.
Your application will be buried
in sand. You leave him
in his cool suit
low on the desert floor.

THE GOALTENDER

When the great Jacques Plante got cut
in Detroit by a puck in the face
he called for the protective mask
no man had seen.

The coach refused but when Jacques
skated out for the final period
he wore the mask and stood
in goal like a tall
lone pole in the wilderness.

On his mask was a map of Chicoutimi.
The Saguenay River poured cold
up the wing at Delvechio, at Howe
and at little Normie Ullman from Edmonton
who'd never seen such a Quebecois.

Pucks flew towards the mask
like geese. But the Wings
failed to score. They were afraid

of the mask he never removed
of the face they could never touch.

Sundown reflected
on the surface of Quebec. Jacques Plante
was all three stars that night.

IF LAFLEUR NEVER PLAYS AGAIN

I babble on
forever in a motion like his.

Let the public be mine.
Let my sisters fill the stands
and chant *Guy! Guy!* Let the faces rise
in tiers of joy and the bodies
of my team-mates crowd around.

I have crossed the frontier of finesse
to the white-blue zone of adulation where
at checkpoints of golden-haired
publicity directors I stop
and their prose turns to flowers
their memories to light.
My ice is my office. Off ice
I am nothing but a mass of winter air
in a thousand dollar coat.
I do not fear injury. My hair
is famous from Moscow to Nanaimo.
I'm thirty-three.

But now I've lost something
on the wing, in the heart.
In their eyes they could see me
grow smaller. Two goals
in twenty games won't keep me

here forever. Soon
I'll paint blue lines
on my face and grow pale
alone at center ice.

THE MAIL DOG OF EMMA LAKE

I saw a dog, while I paddled,
in a coat of government red.
He paddled too in his dog way —
frantic in body below
the surface of the lake
and earnest in face above.
Part of his face was a packet of mail
neatly sealed, I could see, and stamped
with the visage of Queen Elizabeth.

He glanced only
a moment at me in passing.
His eyes were a wobbly brown.
I stopped the canoe
and took a bearing.
South by south-west
I hollered. His soggy ears
perked in brief acknowledgment.

Of course he knows
what he's doing. He does it
five times a week.
They simply wring him out
at the other end, re-load
and send him back to water
for the return swim.

One day, let us hope,
they'll bring him around by truck.

Robert Hilles was born in Kenora, Ontario. He is a graduate of the University of Calgary where he lives teaches Computer Programming. He was awarded the 1994 Governor General's Award for Poetry for *Cantos from a Small Room*. He has published books of poetry regularly since 1980.

MY FATHER WAITS

My father waits in the country for my daughter to visit. He draws her pictures with love holds her in a chair by the window. Light settling into their pores. I can see his passion. His eyes heavy with the sight of the world. Awkwardly he sings to Breanne. The words wrong. His rough face does not frighten her. She smiles as if a different beauty were her preference. They are both larger than the space they occupy.

Beneath this house, there is a river; I can hear the water trickle as it oozes its dance through the blindness of earth. My father's eyes divine the path of the river pointing to various places where it has begun to weaken the foundation. When Breanne cries, he lifts her gently from her discomfort. I wait to catch my father asleep, to watch him swim peacefully in the river he imagines.

AFTER YOU SLEEP I SLEEP

When I went to wake you, I found you sitting in your crib. I was surprised to find you already awake, so quiet, as though you knew I was still sleeping. And I saw you differently. Not as my small daughter, too fragile yet for this complicated world. But as one who knows how your father sleeps

without any trees in his dreams. How some days he is too
tired to hear you cough at night. His pillow hiding his face
like a mask. This morning I could not speak to you my head
still filled with your solitude. Someday you will kiss me a
certain way and I will know that my years are more a
hindrance than an aid. I will know that your eyes see all the
trees I cannot dream. Forgive my hands as they lifted you
this morning from your peace. I cannot explain yet why I did
that. Or why this poem will not let me speak of it now.
Content to confuse as only words and poems can.

STUMBLINGS

He stumbles in after a day of drinking
and I am angry from worrying that he
was lost in Calgary, a strange city for him, or
worse that he was beaten up and robbed in one
of the seedy bars he seeks out.
My father drinks until the pain disappears.
He tells himself the same
stories until he passes out. His strength
is held inside as in a small clay pot.

This winter when he came to visit
I noticed for the first time how
he walks bent over. His tired eyes caved-in
against the light. Every morning he
shovelled the walk or talked to our neighbours
about the bush. I know he can't leave there
and sometimes I am a stranger — out of focus.
In the city, there is too much cement
and all the trout are gone from the Bow River.

He doesn't hear the screams beyond
the walls of the guest bedroom. Instead, love exists

in some other twisted and exaggerated way.
He holds my hand after a day of too much drinking,
and I cannot explain to him the worthiness of his life.

We try to protect one another,
to understand how each violin string
rejects the darkness, to find again
the lights of the world held in a steady
state. I dream of physicists who try to tell
the particles apart. The world frozen in
a tragic order. The chaos more human
than anything. The behaviour of children and
parents equalled by the tragedy of love.

I can only think about one thing at a time.
My mind tired from the fighting, from too many nights
trying to avoid the glare of the TV and his
still eyes. The terror always there. Modern
folktales surrounding us and holding us apart.
I cannot make myself love his contradictions,
yet I am nothing but words that have good intentions,
safe, clean and acceptable.
I want praise and a place to sleep where the
anger does not last all night. I can hear
him walking around in the dark, bumping into my
old typewriter, left too close to the top of
the stairs. In another time I would have
been frightened by his stumblings.
Now I can only guess why he suffers
himself so much.

Our lives more than boundaries apart.
Sometimes we are father and son. Other times,
our purposes are a paradox of wonder and disbelief.
These are hard times between
the beginning and ending of a world.

THIS POEM WILL NOT HARM YOU

It contains only gentle words.
There are no death squads
waiting to claim you between
the syllables. The sounds of
explosions and death are faint
and belong to someone else's
composition You can travel
safely here. It is quiet; rest
between the despair and loss.
Flowers grow carefully in this
poem. Their scents linger
through the rhythm of the
words. Turn each page lightly.
Surrender only as your tongue
imagines its taste. This poem
conquers nothing. Attacks
nothing. It shrinks from
aggression, from arguments,
jagged voices. Turn the page
lightly. Streets in this poem
are filled with music. Even the
dead are light; floating
without the unfamiliar failure
of the grave. Turn the page
lightly. When you finish this
poem, sleep; think only of gods
and what you would like to ask
them. This poem holds no claim
on you, but release it gently.
Others have been tortured for
such thoughts. This poem doesn't care

about the colour of your skin or what
personal atrocities you have witnessed.
Release it gently. It belongs to
you now. There is one final image.
Read it aloud.
One letter at a time.

The poet writes only half the poem. A good poem entices the reader to complete the poem with his own voice, thoughts and feelings, eyes and ears. The journey starts with the first verb and leads to a landscape where all things are one and equal, where thoughts and feelings meet, embrace, make love.

— George Whipple

Doris Hillis was born in England. She came to Canada in 1955 and studied at the University of Manitoba and the University of British Columbia. A teacher by profession, she taught at high school and university level. For many years Hillis lived on a grain farm south of Macklin, Saskatchewan and now lives in Saskatoon.

DAUGHTERS

As I reached my twenties
(with a shrug of the shoulders
and excitement in my heart)
I set out to seek new latitudes

The mother I left
has lived more than half a lifetime
without me
She has grown old wearied
by the years
I grieve never being with her
never being there to ease the tedium
of her shut-in days
On every visit when we part
I see in her eyes
that clubbed-down look

And now my daughter
has reached her twenties
full of the zing and sass of youth
her temper like tinder
brimming with wild dreams
and brash impatience

She spurns my middle age fears
and with a shrug of the shoulders
answers the siren call

STORMHORSES

Under blind of night
black stallion   steelgrey mares
jostle and chafe
until the circling drove
breaks
Hurricane horses   red eyes bared
stream   silver   pewter
across the sky
Slash of ironshod hoof
strikes flame   Forked light
leaps high
They wheel in their rage
heads upflung   manes
sheeting back   mouths
lathered white

THE WAIT

I'm ninety-eight
When I was born Queen Victoria
was on the throne of England
How can I tell you what it's like
to be old?

I have watched my body age:
arms grow pretzel
frail and skin turn toady
nails coarsen to yellow claws

My eyes are bleared
I cannot see the print of books
details of photographs
I am always beyond earshot
beyond the elusive shape of words
My legs have stiffened to brittle sticks
As I walk I tremble   clench
the arms of nurses
I am led   lifted   sponged   changed   fed
dressed like a doll   and left

If people come I spell
the contours of their faces with my fingertips
Sometimes I know them
and sometimes lose them in the
mazes of my mind   and then
nothing matters any more
Nothing and nobody

IDEA FOR A POEM

It's a seed given

And the soil must be prepared
to spur its growth:
tilled to a soft loam
lightened by the aeration
of earthworms
made mealy and rich
from residues of
other years other harvests

It needs a gardener
always in attendance
meticulously pruning
the sturdy plant

that thrusts green shoots
towards the sky
dreaming within itself
a perfect blossom

HE WAS 21

They discharged him
from the army
honourably they said
returned him to his wife
and family

He was 21
his brain maggoted
by memories of war

His wife said
she couldn't stand his rocking
his beseeching hands
nor the way at night
he clawed his own grey flesh

They took him quietly
to a veteran's hospice
and when his mind caved in
moved him to an asylum

Poems often begin in memory and end in discovery.

— Glen Sorestad

Lewis Horne was born in Mesa, Arizona, and educated at Arizona
State University and the University of Michigan. He has taught Eng-
lish at the University of Michigan, at Colorado College and at the
University of Saskatchewan. He lives in Saskatoon, Saskatchewan.

WATCHING MY DAUGHTERS DRIVE OFF FOR UNIVERSITY

Suitcases, boxes and bags, a knapsack.
The Peugeot piled so high it looks
like a toy car, tucked full as a sock
at Christmas. Then with children loaded,
down the morning street it moves
before the neighbours rise. It took

some magic to accomplish this
departure. Not in the loading alone.
But in the coil of days that are left
behind, echoing, like a boarded-
over movie house with the reel
in storage. Alive in the gritty

air, as much alive as the smell
of popcorn, are witnesses
of Saturdays. With them, I think
of summer, years, the forms of what
you were and are as though I watch
a picture show I had some part in,

cast, and sold the tickets for —
took my cut before you went.
There is transparency to life —
and mystery — and light projects
a new assurance as it fills
the day and the car I watch from the lawn.

Bruce Hunter was born in Calgary and later moved to Ontario. He graduated from York University and taught Creative Writing at York and at the Banff School of Fine Arts. He teaches English at Seneca College in Toronto and lives in Stratford, Ontario. He has published books of poetry and fiction.

JUNE 23, 1973

You found her,
you and your buddy Tom,
abandoned in an alley.
The torn ragtop, back window gone,
four flat tires, but potential there.

A few weeks shy of seventeen, swigging beer
bought by someone you asked
outside the vendor's on 37th Street.
Light in a bottle, power and speed.
Nothing can stop you.

The guy lets you have her
for a hundred bucks.
TR 6, fast as a rumour.
Tires hawked from the Goodyear.
You bring her in.
Norris, the shop teacher, looking on;
other guys in Automotives jealous,
rich kid's car.
All of you,
calling only one thing in your lives, her.

The prom three weeks away.
You were the guys without dates.

Fingernails greasy with lube;
tiny road maps of grime on your fingers.
And shop talk a front against loneliness.
Valve jobs, headers, cams.
Not engines you were talking,
but love.
Too shy to ask Charlene, at the Dairy Queen,
for anything more.

You pulled the engine, rebored her.
New rings, gaskets.
Rolling into the sunshine.
Then down to the wash on 33rd,
plates borrowed from Norris' Malibu.
A few times by the drive of the D.Q.
Charlene looking *your* way now.

When you pull the front end,
a pin sheared;
front wheel barely on.
Dealer out of stock.
Wrecker's not much better
in a town where everyone drives Fords.

What to do? You and Tom, your beer cooling;
while you huck stones at River Park.
Thursday.   The prom tomorrow night.
Wire, he says.   Yeah, wire.
Don't tell Norris.
Friday afternoon the pin replaced with wire.
Twisting it with pliers.
There, it won't drop.

You can hardly believe it.
New plates your brother bought.
You and Tom take her up the hill climb road
to Broadcast Hill.   To the parking spot

under the radio tower over the city,
but the lot is empty before sundown.

So you cruise the bypass road.
She needs no coaxing to hit sixty.
Letting her down easy,
to the river again.
Your turf after dark.

Sometimes the rich kids, frat rats and their girls
in pleated skirts, come in convoys.
Goofs, greasers, they taunt you.
Then it's chains slapped on car hoods.
Sometimes a knuckle to nose, bone crushing
on the steps of the school. As far as it gets,
all that rage. Tonight you forget about that.

Elsewhere, others are getting ready too.
Corsages sweating in the fridge.
Dresses on the bedspread, new shoes.
You and Tom and her.
The beer is better this time.
You're confident.   This power.
Won't let him take the wheel.
Later, you say, when I'm pissed.

As the sun goes down, you build a fire.
And the other loners arrive, drinking beer,
traces of their cigarettes in the dark.
Someone asks how fast she goes.
You hadn't thought of that.
Like a challenge.

By eleven, you're on the road,
Zeppelin on the tape,
bottled light in your eyes.
Few cars this time of night.
Cops all down in the city.

The tach pops with each shift.
80-95-100
She hums.
You're soaring with her,
a road race machine that corners at 90,
into the curves.

Cutting shorter and faster
But you forget something.
The pin.

No one will say anything
until after the prom.
Charlene's there, not even noticing
you're not.
Later a few people say they wondered.

And what you couldn't have known.
How she flipped three times, the cops said.
When she lost the wheel.
Sheared a power pole.
The first news gentle.
Days pass, then the gross details.
First, through the windshield to your shoulders,
held by the dash, then snapped back again.
Your stubborn head.

And Tom they found in the bushes.
The wheel meshed in a tree.
Kids came in processions,
even the rich kids.   Mortality
somehow linking you.
Too late.   Vague skidmarks.
The pole already replaced.   A few oil spots
fragrant with sage dust.   No bloodstains.
Wanting something
to be there.   To mark it.

One. Young men and women with degrees in English literature, living in fashionably seedy districts, writing poetry in sexually inclusive language about rape, murder, and wife-beating, all of which happens to other people.

Two. In urban clubrooms, churches, and universities, anyone engaged in politically correct discourse on pornography, violence, or Nicaragua. This is the True Story, the poem that can be written.

Three. My mother with a knife. This is where the definition gets personal. I am seventeen years old. She steps between my sister and my alcoholic father. That night I leave home. One year later she does. Something Margaret Atwood knows nothing about.

Four. In divorce court, the judge, two lawyers, all of them male. My mother gets one dollar a year and social assistance. My father buys a new house.

Five. My teenaged brothers in jail. For minor offences, none of them malicious. On the other side of the thick plexiglas window, their faces bruised. The elevator in the police station stopped between floors. A telephone book applied to the abdomen, the ribs. Tonight is Friday. Monday morning there will be no visible damage before the judge.

Six. The police visit my mother looking for my brothers. It is 4 a.m. This happens often. My sisters are stopped for identification checks. This too happens often. This is what they do to the lower classes in your country.

Tonight somewhere in the suburbs you are talking about us. Some of you are writing poems, taking donations, or making a film. You feel okay about this.

And my mother now goes to your churches. She has forgiven you. I have not.

SLOW LEARNER

1.

the way the kid told me
working for the summer
hometown Standard, Alberta
your basic five elevator
one drugstore no bar town
on a spur line near Drumheller
town foreman got him pruning poplar
gave him enough work
to keep out of trouble
the three days he was gonna be gone
prune em up good, top em off here
pointing somewhere near his belt
three days later the foreman was back
all over town, not a tree
higher than the belt on his pants

2.

this winter the kid's working on my crew
we're pruning young cottonwood
which stand about chest high
each tree's got two main stems
might look like two
if you didn't know

he's down on the other end
when i decide to see how he's doing

he's gone and cut down every second stem
figuring the other one was a sucker

we kick snow over the stumps
cut down the other half
so the boss won't ever figure
there was a tree here

for the sake of history i'm hoping
we'll both be gone before the snow

SNOW PLOW DRIVER'S DREAM

it's the crew boss: *big storm last night*
so we're calling the crews in early
and me in from my dream
of a skeletal ship in distant clouds
where she holds aloft a single card
she is not my mother or a lover
the card is the queen of spades

past the curtains in frosted windows
day is a ghostridden horizon
trees sway in windy choreography
i hear laughing roar
as she cocks her dark head
lifts haughtily skirts in storm
today i will watch my roads
for the scuffled tracks of a black dancer
that card she holds is mine

FOR MY BROTHER DANIEL

"BENCHMARK"
starting point of a survey

driving down from survey school
on highway 41 north of Battle River
miles of uninterrupted bush
save on small graveyard
with its white framed mission
beside it tombstones
high-centered in sweetgrass
these final shapes of ancestry
dust and bones without light
faces in the family album
funeral wreaths of ox-eyed daisy
and yarrow mark their roads

"SURVEYOR"
an explorer, one who determines size
shapes, ownership, and boundaries

or as legitimate history might have you believe
oldest of seven children, my sister tells me
years later, as my mother told only her
there was one other born before all this
before the legal marriage
my mother held him long enough
to name him Daniel
she was told only that
the couple was from Edmonton

is he alive/well my bastard brother
an engineer or a hockey player
some hero in a country song

oblivious to a brother
more surveyor than poet
who drives these roads searching
for the shapes of the ancestor we share

i met a man today
from Edmonton, my height
with the same crooked teeth
dark laugh and eyes caustic
he too was a surveyor

Writing is fishing around. If you just sit down and fish bits of dream and discovery and insight swirl at the end of your focus and it's exciting experimentally putting it together to rhythm.

— *Chris Collins*

Gary Hyland is a native Moose Jaw writer, columnist, editor and occasional lecturer for the University of Regina. He was a founding member of the Thunder Creek Co-op, the Sage Hill Writing Experience, Art School Saskatchewan, and the Festival of Words. He is a graduate of the University of Saskatchewan and has published poetry for more than twenty years.

THE DOCTOR

No more boxers for me.

Bar room brawlers,
that's another story.
They don't train
to destroy people.
No one pays to watch
a couple of drunks
demolish furniture.

Four and a half hours
inside this kid's head
and *I'll* fight anyone
who calls this *sport*.

Prize fighting?
You want to know
this kid's prize?
Bifrontal craniotomy,
three subdural hematomas,
possible embolisms,
possible skull fracture,
total left hemiplegia.

Let me translate.
If he ever wakes up
half life in the cabbage patch,
maybe complete loss
of his whole left side,
years of therapy
so he can shuffle,
drool and gawk about.

No more boxers for me.
I'm a neurosurgeon
not a bloody botanist.

SPORTS ILLUSTRATED PHOTO

Black and white. Late afternoon. Staged. The sun, weak with winter, is in a haze behind the man, but his shadow topples like a victim to his right. The tracks must have been shuffled through the snow, not one distinct. They stop in mid-pasture, the snow beyond, broken only by a few frozen stems of weeds, sweeps into a black stretch of barren trees. The easy wind sifts like distant applause. Before the trees, a four-rail fence. No ropes now for Muhammad Ali in this larger ring, puffy-cheeked, alone on his farm in scarf and overcoat, coached by a photographer, squinting cloudy-eyed into lights. The tremors of his illness stilled by the quick shutter. The old gang who used to make and share the glory, gone — flung from Vegas to Maine, rummy rags and death to other vestibules of fame. Fabulous times, even when the reflexes flagged and the fists were pumped with novocaine. Even when the beatings began. Toasted by kings and presidents, entire floors in swanky hotels, the best of the best blazing fifteen years. Now all the colour is in the barn where he keeps framed photos and paintings of the bright-eyed bee and butterfly days. The glitzy robes, the entourage in jewels, the gorgeous wives. Showing the pictures to the visitor, he notices in nearly every one his almost pretty face is streaked with pigeon shit. Slowly he turns them to the wall. One by one. He walks outdoors. Into black and white.

A SAFE AND EASY THING

Don't stop reading, Mildred.
There's no need to be afraid.
This is not a poem. Pretend
you can hear me speaking,
pretend I am in a small room
far away playing the music
pictures happy in your head.

See? You don't need to think.
The words are small and easy,
the lines are short, the print
large, like an advertisement.
Nothing will happen to you,
nothing to buy or believe or give,
like pudding, pudding on a spoon.

No one will ask what this means.
No one will care you've read it.
It is almost over and nothing
has happened. Not the sniff
of a mention of something odd,
nothing shifty, nothing fancy,
not one unpleasant anything.

You can be proud of yourself.
Should there be a power failure,
should the bubble puddings stop,
in the cough and shuffle silence
here's something nice you can say
to your friends who never read,
not even signs or recipes.

Once I read a whole page of words
that my husband set into chunks.
It was easy, really, very easy.
It was about itself and me
and I could forget it right away.
That's something to flaunt safely.
It's not as if you'd read a poem.

OUT OF HABIT

They discuss things in the car driving
nowhere up and down the streets so that
if one of them screams or weeps the kids
won't be disturbed. The kids are at home
watching a Disney flick in the family room.
She is not sure how much she will tell him
whether to mention the other man or maybe
just the job having to keep her away.

He sits too erect, arms stiff, hands tight.
Tonight is different in a way he doesn't know.
What has happened? What is going on?
Everything he says begins with *but*.
It's raining. He can't find the wiper switch.

She wishes she'd brought some cigarettes. Now
that she has started she must finish the job.
Somewhere in this purse there are cigarettes.
His rational spiel is almost over. She
breathes deeply, mumbles that she doesn't want
to be married. She has no reasons. Just that.
There is no traffic, no one on the sidewalks.
She looks at house lights through wet glass.
How many of them she wonders, how many.

He pulls into a closed service station.
Trying to expel the pain, coughing, crying, he
doubles over, slams himself against the door.
She lights a cigarette and takes a slow drag.
He looks like one of those black and white
films, the old ones where nothing much happens.

He gets out, walks a while in the cool rain,
over and over slamming wet fist into wet palm.

Her breath mists the windows. He gets in,
turns on the defogger, the headlights, the wipers.
Out of habit the car returns them to the house.

THE FIRST MOON OF MOOSE JAW

We stash our clothes in Scrawny's car
and go bare-ballin down by the dam
me, Scrawny, Zip and Magoo
After, we dress in the back seat
Magoo, as usual, still in the creek
and the sun meltin the upholstery
A few horn blasts and he waddles up
sloshes over Zip and starts dryin
hunched-up like a pregnant walrus
Zip takes exception to be being drowned
and they start shovin back and forth

Before long Zip pins Magoo's head
and somehow pushes the poor bugger
so his rump's jammed outa the window
till the bulgin flesh spills out
and sizzles on the hot chrome trim
Magoo screams and squirms first-rate
but Zip's got him pretzeled real snug
Scrawny he never misses a good chance

so he starts the Dodge and we light out
with a windowful of Magoo's pink cheeks
bouncin like a coupala baby pigs

Right away I can see where we're headed
cause there's a mess of Holy Rollers
havin a prayer orgy down the road
There musta been maybe three hundred
fryin in their shiny Sunday outfits
around some thumper on an oil-drum stage

Then we roars up like Judgement Day
and Scrawny leans out and hollers
Behold, brothers, the face of Lucifer
He cuts through the field to give em
a close-up wide-angle view so to speak
then floors her and we dust outa there
horn ablastin and Magoo ascreamin
and us three roarin like all royal hell

ELAINE'S SWIMMERS

Each week she watched the swimmers
the glisten of their shoulder muscles
the lean sweep of torsos
the twining sinews of their legs
the trunks tight over small buttocks
making a snug curl of the bulge in front —
the beautiful anointed bodies
hair sleek, faces fresh and grinning.

But when she wed she chose the earth
married a realtor, had Disneyland daughters,
split-level headaches and two-car quarrels,
golf on Tuesdays and drinks with the girls.
In the sand-trap glare at the Country Club
she blinks away mirages full of swimmers.

TELEMACHUS

The old man shoves off.
Again. 20 years
of globetrotting
ain't enough.
A change of shirts
and ships and good-bye.

Considerate guy.
My whole youth shot
guarding *his* palace
running *his* lands
and he says *Good job*
son. Seeya around.
Really. Consider it.

Off with his cronies
adventure junkies
perpetual tourists
to leap the sheer edge
of all existence.

All people cheer!
That really burns me
Oh, isn't he brave!
Not gonna rust up.

Grabbing experience.
All that rah-rah crap.

Experience *for* what?
Processed when?
Talk about your un-
examined life.
If he slobbered
in a bar that long
they'd wag their heads
and call him a turd.

But Alfred Lord writes
this nifty poem
which grad speakers
go berserk quoting
forever after.
Well here's a rhyme
that's more with it:
a hero on the roam
means a busted home.

Like it's a real drag
when your old man's
an adolescent.

In poetry there must always be room for the unforeseen, the unexpected, or the poem lies dead upon the page.

— H.C. Dillow

Sherry Johnson was born in Craik, Saskatchewan, and brought up in Eastend. Sherry studied at the University of Saskatchewan and currently lives in Saskatoon.

FULL LUNAR ECLIPSE

For a moment
the sky holds a perfect yin-yang,
the moon coupling with the earth's shadow

and me embracing a memory
by the cold, still river.
Through the moon the earth

darkens my face.
Suddenly I am a veiled woman
with no-one to mourn for.

PSYCHOTHERAPY

This is what becomes of you, at 4 a.m.
I am thinking of the split-triangled enigma
of the moth, how two scalenes are really
a circle, 360 mystical degrees.
I remember that's what the textbooks say.

I think of this, Nurse Cratchet doing rounds
and me still awake, pretending to sleep.
The day's revelations goad my mind:
the faces of those I hadn't conjured in years
thaw before me. Here they are simply icons,
part of everyone else's pain.

So I explore this, and the faces become
less human, less tangible, and I am left

with that deceiving soft sound of footsteps
down the antiseptic hallway —

The faces dissolve, coagulate into
one enemy. A head is formed,
sometimes a woman, sometimes a man.
The infliction of pain isn't exclusive to gender.

So it's 4 a.m.
I am positive that Nurse Cratchet feels innocent.
People have inflicted pain on her.
Once, when she was a child
someone did unmentionable things to her.
They said *never tell*, and she didn't.
She refused to become a victim.

Which of us is better off?
Here in my bed, past 6 o'clock now, a head forms,
duplicating row on row like a precise cancer.
Unsure of the enemy, I try to scrape the heads
off these postage sheets in my skull.
I try to remember the art of detachment.

The dark diffuses.
Outside, the first sparkle of morning
from the night. The lamposts' timers
shut themselves off in the dusk.

The moths glide down, becoming
rings of light.

*Readers of poetry should not be fazed by difficulty. They should expect
a challenging journey and be prepared to expend time and effort, like
avid climbers before a mountain peak.*

— Doris Hillis

MEDITATION 3

Patrick Lane

Were it not for the sonnet, the set forms of verse, we should
all be at the mercy of genius.

— Oscar Wilde

What I am saying is that, in the long run, to break the rules,
you must know *about* the rules.

— Jorge Luis Borges

I would like to give you a sonnet written by Weldon Kees who
died of an apparent suicide in 1955 in San Francisco. This poem
had a great effect on me when I first read it in 1969 when I was
staying at John Gill's farm a few miles from Ithaca, New York (John
Gill was the publisher of *New: American & Canadian Poetry*, a
seminal magazine of the period and the first and only American
magazine to juxtapose as equals the poetry of the two nations). I
became fascinated by the poem and read and reread it, thinking it
was the content of the poem that had so moved me. I was still a
young poet even though I had been writing for more than ten
years. It was only after several weeks that I realized I was looking
at a sonnet. This came as a shock. It had never occurred to me
that a modern poet would bother to write in an old form. I thought
free verse had liberated us all from such a traditional form. But
perhaps I should give you the poem. It is called "For My Daughter".

> *Looking into my daughter's eyes I read*
> *Beneath the innocence of morning flesh*
> *Concealed, hintings of death she does not heed.*
> *Coldest of winds have blown this hair, and mesh*
> *Of seaweed snarled these miniatures of hands;*
> *The night's slow poison, tolerant and bland,*
> *Has moved her blood. Parched years that I have seen*
> *That may be hers appear: foul, lingering*
> *Death in certain war, the slim legs green.*

Or, fed on hate, she relishes the sting
Of other's agony; perhaps the cruel
Bride of a syphlitic or a fool.
These speculations sour in the sun.
I have no daughter. I desire none.

It was because of this poem that I decided seriously to begin an exploration of form. It was not that I had ignored form, but that I had been struggling for ten years with free verse and while I had occasionally succeeded in writing a fairly good poem in the form I really didn't know what I was doing. Most of what I constructed was unconscious, a poetry that was informed by a tradition drilled into me in high school English classes and further back, the oral recitations of my mother who knew thousands of lines of traditional verse, poetry she had to memorize when she was a girl in the early part of the century. This tradition, the verse of Tennyson and Byron and others that my mother was wont to sing, and the poems of my high school anthologies, singular examples that were supposed to cover an era, a century, a millenium, was for me like looking at the sky, seeing a few stars in early evening, and not questioning the darkness that surrounded them. I had no basis in the tradition. My problem was that I didn't have a context for free verse. I believed, as only a young mid-century poet would, that Pound and Eliot had freed us from the sterile bonds of the past, the laboured repetitions of prescribed forms. I didn't question it. This was received knowledge, something my peers and I parroted to each other in bars and bedrooms. I didn't know that unconsciously I was using rhythms and cadences, patterns and figures that had a history that went back into the tradition. I thought I was breaking new ground with my poems but, of course, I was not. The following poem, written in 1967 or 1968, a year before I read Weldon Kees' sonnet, is an example of this. The cadence and the rhymes were pleasing to my ears but I didn't know *why* they pleased me! The poem is called "For Ten Years".

Tonight the moon slants cold into the snow.
Ice shudders on the glass and suddenly alone
I'm aware of windows. Was it you who told me
you were gone? Beyond the snow
light rides thin as a broken bow
without a hand to guide it. From this hour
darkness comes shrill as a dying bird.

One night in the north you lay in my arms
and wept for a crying bird. In the morning
you found him dead on the window-sill.
His beak was a crust of ice
that melted as you breathed.
When I threw him away, he didn't fly.
That country of snow we lived in
was a cushion for owls to walk on.
Birds don't understand windows.
They never did.

The last two lines of the poem came from a visit to Dorothy
Livesay's cottage on the Sunshine Coast in the town of Sechelt.
Seymour Mayne and I were visiting for the day. While we were
there a bird flew into the reflecting glass of a window. Seymour,
a man who had grown up in Montreal, had never seen a bird do
this and when he asked me why it had done such a thing I replied,
"Birds don't understand windows." And then, as an afterthought,
added rather ruefully, given I had just gone through a divorce and
was quite unhappy, "They never did." Seymour said to me, "Now
that's poetry!" The next day I wrote the poem quoted above and
was quite unconscious that the first line was a pentameter line. It
sounded right to me, though why I couldn't have told you, any
more than I could have explained the ensuing cadences and
rhythms.

What was important was the discovery of Weldon Kees' son-
net and my surprise when I realized it was a sonnet. I felt I had

been lying to myself for more than a decade and that, if I really wanted to be a poet, I should learn *how* to write. That, rather than slavishly imitating the modern masters, the two generations immediately preceding my own, I should go back into the tradition and read the old masters, John Donne, Robert Browning, William Wordsworth, William Butler Yeats, Emily Dickinson, Andrew Marvell, William Blake, Samuel Taylor Coleridge, and, of course, Shakespeare. *How* did they achieve the effects in their poems? What was I to do with Emund Waller's,

> Go, lovely rose!
> Tell her that wastes her time and me
>   That now she knows,
> When I resemble her to thee,
> How sweet and fair she seems to be.

What was I to do with Shakespeare's lines, "Desiring this man's art and that man's scope,/With what I most enjoy contented least," and Donne's, "Go and catch a falling star,/Get with child a mandrake root,/Tell me where all past years are,/Or who cleft the Devil's foot," and how had such lines written in past centuries affected the way I wrote now? Why, if I thought such lines wonderful, was I refusing to learn from them? And more than that, was there a way I could incorporate such form into my own poetry. If there was a tradition why had I studiously ignored it in favour of the contemporary? And I had *studiously* ignored it. I had sneered at the romantics, Shelley and Byron and Keats. I had turned instead toward what many of my contemporaries insisted was the only poetry to emulate, that of the Black Mountain School of writers, Charles Olson, Robert Creeley, Denise Levertov, and others. It was not that these people were bad writers. On the contrary, they were very fine writers indeed. It was simply that I had chosen too narrow a field to work in. I broke away from my contemporaries and spent the next five years studying the masters. If I wanted to be a good writer, I thought back then, I had much to learn. I still believe that and still believe I have much to learn.

As Borges said when he was seventy-two, "In spite of my failures, I still keep trying to be a poet."

When Borges says that free verse is a very difficult form for a beginning writer he is saying it is made more difficult for that young writer who has no grounding in the tradition of English literature. The antecedents of free verse go back to the sixteenth century. To know who we are we must understand where we have come from; to write new poems we must first understand how new an old poem can be and how it informs everything we do. Perhaps then we might understand the lines from Al Purdy's poem, "Wilderness Gothic",

> *That picture is incomplete, part left out*
> *that might alter the whole Dürer landscape:*
> *gothic ancestors peer from medieval sky,*
> *dour faces trapped in photograph albums escaping*
> *to clop down iron roads with matched greys:*
>
> *An age and a faith moving into transition,*
> *the dinner cold and new-baked bread a failure,*
> *deep woods shiver and water drops hang pendant,*
> *double yoked eggs and the house creaks a little -*
> *Something is about to happen. Leaves are still.*
> *Two shores away, a man hammering in the sky.*
> *Perhaps he will fall.*

A student at Columbia University once said to Borges, who had encouraged students to work in traditional forms, "I can't imagine writing sonnets or rhyming couplets." Borges' response was, "I don't think you can possibly discard all of the past. If you do, you run the risk of discovering things that have already been discovered. This comes from a lack of curiosity. Aren't you curious about the past? Aren't you curious about your fellow poets in this century? In the last century? And in the eighteenth century? Doesn't John Donne mean anything to you? Or Milton?"

I think the argument Borges and countless others have made is that free verse, taken by itself without any fundamental practice in earlier forms (both in reading and writing) becomes a most difficult form to master. The casual student assumed that free verse implies that anything goes, that any arbitrary collection of sentence fragments arranged in an ordered ladder down the page constitutes a poem. Nothing is farther from the truth. The student must think his way into the tradition and learn *how* a poem is made. To write a sonnet is no easy thing, any more than to write a sestina or villanelle, yet to attempt to do so is to learn how difficult it is to write within prescribed form. And that is a *given* form, a comfort zone with its rigid cadences and rhymes. How much more difficult when the student must bring form willy-nilly out of himself? It is no easy task to compose a poem in a traditional form, let alone do it in a free or open form. One only has to read the masters to know that.

I would like to end this with a poem of my own called "How the Heart Stinks With Its Devotions", dedicated to "the brothers D'Amour and Johnny Gringo", friends I spent a weekend with in 1975 in Prince George. We had argued the night about poetry and writing, form and content, this poet and that poet, until we all fell asleep, exhausted by the passion of our conversation and discussion, sometimes violent, sometimes peaceful and harmonious. I woke early in the morning, hungover and dreary. To give myself some brief, intangible sanity I began reading an anthology of English Literature over a cup of coffee and two ounces of scotch, happy my friends were still asleep and happy I could have these hours alone with my thoughts before I climbed into my truck and drove the hundreds of miles back to the coast. As I read, a poem came drifting in on my thought. I leave you with it.

HOW THE HEART STINKS WITH ITS DEVOTIONS

How the heart stinks with its devotions —
Rot my wisdom, I am drowned
In the poisonous storms of the mind.
To remember dying
Buried in the surge of the dance.
Empty your eyes of all save form.
It is the green perfection of the space
A leaf includes in its growing,
The delicate birth baffled by the wind.
Ah, heart, I cannot scorn the armies of your pain.
It is night, air, and I am drunk again on words.
One stone would be enough.
One leaf a feast.

Patrick Lane was born in Nelson, B.C. He has published more than twenty books of poetry and fiction. He has received every literary prize and award in Canada including the Governor General's Award for Poetry in 1978 for *New and Selected Poems*. His work has been translated into many languages. He currently teaches at the University of Victoria. He is one of Canada's pre-eminent poets.

Magpie, magpie, do not take a lower branch than this.
Last home I dreamed I was night. Poverty and song.

Autumn. The crabapple drops its small and bitter fruit.
The old attend to their gardens. Under the earth. Love.

The ones who are lost sing longer than the ones who are alone.
Blind at birth, I want you back.

Stay with me, carrion bird.
I am thinking of last leaves. The beauty of beginning.

A bad line, breaking wrong, hurts the eye.
How much worse the ear?

A mouth in a tree cries forgive, forgive.
Like a body fallen on a bed. A white bed. A body.

Forgive me.
I was going nowhere and going anyway.

The eyes that name you have no tongue.
Old roads. The arrival in time. Witnesses.

The line is doubtful. The meaning is clear. Endure.
We remember a boy in wind, a bell in an open field.

Full moon, I love you, your rising and your falling.
The cedar wax-wings are drunk. Frost on the berries.

Give of your grace. The sun forgives.
I am afraid of nothing. Blow wind. The bell is lonely.

The new world. The anvil. Water in deep well.
Between your hips the only parasite is me.

Don't shake your hoary locks at me. I am still hungry.
Laughter. How the mind works, works, works.

Widow-maker.
Charm-breaker.

Too many questions.
This is what is meant by noise. Tell me! Tell me!

Then turn, good friend.
These are your stars. The slivered moon rising.

I am a poet and artist concerned with verbal and visual poetic imagery.
The importance of poetry and visual art is that these are forms of
communication at various levels of meaning.

— Helen Hawley

William Latta was born in East Liverpool, Ohio. He is a graduate
of the University of Nebraska. William was a Fullbright Scholar
and has taught English at the University of Lethbridge where he
is presently a Professor Emeritus.

A GOOD FRIDAY BIRTH

In the sun-mottled morning,
Her belly heaving with hurt,
She washed, baked bread, tried to rest.
Outside: the restlessness of cold and warm,
Contention of promised buds
And stubborn chill.
Altogether, it was an appropriate day.

At noon, half-hold of sunlight broke,
Gave way to sleet-slashed rain,
And in the interior gloom
She remembered Calvary and death.
The house hushed with mother's sorrow,
With the torment of child,
With sadness, doubt and pain. So much.

The hours of accomplishment passed
And, for the life of her,
She lay locked with death.

Dim skies darkened,
Descended;
Rain gave way to snow.
She worked for breath,
Fought darkness,
Gasped from exhaustion,
Wept.

And in the dark, dead afternoon,
Her child was born.

Shelley A. Leedahl was born in Kyle, Saskatchewan. She studied at the University of Saskatchewan. She is a dynamic member of the Saskatchewan writing community as a poet and fiction writer. She lives in Saskatoon.

WHEN SUMMER SPREADS

When summer spreads her bare brown legs
all the town kids beat it to the lake
in fast cars they'll have totalled off
by the end of the season.

You've gotta grab the few hot ones
and settle down on the beach
with a babe, a beer and some summertime tunes.

This ain't no California, but you can't tell
them that.   These kids forget
this is the north when summer spreads
and they're riding the heat waves,
and if you squint just right, even you will believe
those giant evergreens are palm trees.

BURNING
for Barb

I remember us, so much alike,
so much in love with tough guys
who drove muscle cars and smoked
too much dope. It's easy
to look back, recall faces

brightened by fires at bush parties,
weekends at the lake, the warmth
of our lovers' bare skin.
We were too young to have felt such heat.

I saw your boyfriend slam his fists in your face.
Blood streamed from your nose, through your fingers.
My boyfriend hit me only once; he burned me
without leaving scars.

After high school, you and I grew apart.
If there were letters, I don't remember.
Still, there's one night that binds us.
It was nearly Christmas.   We were driving
to your house on the edge of town.
I still feel the swell of the car,
the heave as we drove over the drunk.
Then us running past the body,
eyes burning in the cold,
our shoes sliding down the icy highway
to the first lighted house.

A FEW WORDS FOR JANUARY

It was such a cold winter, 1985.
We scraped circles off the crystallized dance
on our windows, saw plump white ghosts
sitting in trees across the lane.

It was a beautiful, slow time. A snowed-in time.
I told your father we should name you January,
after the quiet perfection of snow.
No, he said, *you cannot name the child after cold.*

That frozen morning in the third month,
I took a number in the hospital's admissions.

Sat quietly through the feverish child,
the glue-intoxicated woman.
Kept my knees clamped, holding you in.

Your grandmother prayed, said it would be all right.
I could not forgive them, Mother or God,
for a long time, for letting me hope.

It was such a cold winter.
After they took you.
I thought only of replacing
what I had lost; the emptiness
no one would speak of.

This poem is for you, my mysterious one,
cradled warm in my womb for three solid months.
Sleep sweetly, snow angel, with the prettiest,
the coldest name.

SPRING

From my kitchen window
the season is orderly, predictable.
Water floods the black garden,
kids stomp in the luscious earth,
jump from the few icy islands
to where water swells
over rubber boot tops.

I will let them play;
chance pneumonia, long hours of laundry
to see their mud-splashed faces.
They dump pailfuls of water,
and watch the new puddles,
squeeze the dark soil
through their fingers.

Who am I to tell them:
Come out of the garden,
and risk destroying everything
growing and glorious.

MOTHER LOVE

She didn't want to do it but they'd been out of milk for a week
already and the kids needed new boots and the power
company was threatening and the school wanted money for a
lost book and she had to buy medicine for the youngest and
wouldn't it be nice just to wear a new coat that no one else
had already worn

She didn't want to do it but her husband couldn't keep a job
and she'd never been to school and didn't have any skills and
her children needed her at home and she'd only do it once and
no one would ever have to know

She didn't want to do it but there was this man with the nice
smile who'd helped her pay for the groceries and she couldn't
just let him pity her like that

She didn't want to do it but it wasn't so bad after it was over
and he held her for a minute before he gave her the money
and told her about some of his friends

She didn't want to do it but most of them were just ordinary
men and there was only the one who'd hurt her and even then
he'd paid her extra and she couldn't stop now because the rent
just went up and her oldest boy needs glasses and it's nice to
have fresh fruit and some mothers just love too much

SOME DAYS ALL I WANT FROM LIFE
IS A PEANUT BUTTER AND BANANA SANDWICH

The mailman brings another rejection —
the local journal which always buys
my stories and poems, no matter
how bad. My husband receives a letter
from Unemployment Insurance, stating
we owe *them* $912 for an overpayment
they gave us, their mistake.

Yesterday we sold the kids' skates
for $25 and finally had milk
for breakfast. Two days earlier
it had been a joke. I said:
Troy, we have to buy milk,
and he said: *Can't they just have toast*
for breakfast? then realized
we didn't have any bread.
We laughed and laughed.

I wonder how long friends will continue
 to see me, considering how often I evade
their requests to go shopping, see shows,
do lunch. I broke down and told one of them:
        We never go for lunch.
        We don't have the money.
I told her how far beneath the poverty line
we live and she wouldn't look at me
but began crying her own blues,
the mortgage payments of two homes,
something I know nothing, will never
know anything about.

Today all I want from life is a peanut butter
and banana sandwich, but the bread's
for the kids and bananas are expensive.
Today even that's out of reach.

Poetry is the longing we feel for what we don't have, the joy we feel for what we do. Anyone who says they don't like poetry is a liar.

— Dave Margoshes

John Lent is a poet, fiction writer, and songwriter who teaches
Creative Writing and Literature at Okanagan University College
in Vernon. He was born in Antogonish, Nova Scotia, and educated
at the University of Alberta and York University. Lent has been
publishing poetry, fiction, and articles in periodicals in Canada and
abroad for the last twenty years. Lent lives in Vernon, British
Columbia.

ENCLOSED GARDEN, 1

have been tending private gardens instead

pass through the grey film of the door
descend blue stairs armed with clippers
trowels gloves pails rakes a variety of
sprinklers on hoses   the lawnmower

groom lawns and flower beds
plant annuals   a clematis
a virginia creeper

ceremoniously install a tamarisk
a sun-burst locust

trying to break the linear mathematics
of our standard city lot

and yet simultaneously
I attempt to manicure this garden
into another order

we commit this contradiction on ourselves
not as innocent as instinct versus reason

as if contrary selves
perceived alternate beauties
we are at war
growing ourselves chaotically
rearranging   reordering

this garden

is always two photographs of itself
one superimposed upon another

they never match up

these photos

unless a third synthetic self
leans back into this striped canvas chair
stretches its limbs

at peace in this vortex of wills

watches the water whirl round and round

drenching a porous ground with

possibility

PASTORAL #1: ST. ALBERT SIDEROAD, 1961

I see that boy running now down the bevelled sideroad. Running
into the scissored quarter sun's splitting into an unspun fibre the
willow line's twisting loom. The warp and the weft become silvered
greens and golds while the gravel road and its ditches here gain in
deepening charcoals, are rolling now beneath the touch of his feet
in a feast of hay, of mustard seed and clover. A soft dust from the
stones covers running shoes and jeans. The hesitant, funnelling,
August breeze brushes the white tee-shirt against his bony ribs,
shifts the dark blue woolen sweater out behind him, flapping, as he
becomes some kinetic image of his joy, some concretion of all those

abrupt combinations when his heart runs into itself out there,
becomes its elemental moment, blown far, far inside, past
the dusty freckled grin, past the private squinting eyes, past all these
into the landscape where the future dances always: dances the body
in its earth.

*The only way we can realize the landscape the way our mind pictures it
is to empower the ground with words.*

— *Michael Cullen*

Mark Lowey was born in Dauphin, Manitoba, and now lives in Calgary where he works as a journalist. He studied at the University of Calgary and the Southern Alberta Institute of Technology.

IN THE FIELD

In the field
with gopher flankers,
grasshopper ends,
we played football.
I was a one-rule manager:
everybody plays,
even beagle Toby
barking out signals;
little kids afraid of the game
served as wandering goalposts.
Neighbourhood mothers
thought me possessed
or godsent: lining up
their summertime runaways
into ragamuffin defence,
ragtag offence,
racing them to exhaustion.

My peers mocked their way
to dances, backseat touch.
Their eyes shouldered me
against gymnasium walls,
marked me separate.
But in the field
I was never alone.

I stand here years later,
catch shades running patterns
through tall grass;
the sun wobbles
to the shout
of touchdowns, fumbles,
no one is keeping score.

SONS OF ICARUS

Beginning at the myth:
Daedalus and Icarus, confined
to the grey light of Knossos,
sought the sun, designed

wings worthy of an angel.
Down the labyrinth of halls
Daedalus bent upon labour,
Icarus dreamed above walls.

Daedalus feathered flight
with reason, mindful of the heat.
Icarus soared on faith, heedless
of seas beneath his feet.

Father rose on pinions
to the height that freedom brings.
We are sons of son, captives
to half-completed wings.

ICARUS REVISITED

Tar-paper strips flutter
free of the roof,
drape like giant bat wings
over the willow tree.
I could have died
seventeen times today:
stopped shingling and
flung my absurdly winged body
toward the sun.
I would have livened up
a half-dead afternoon
for all the neighbours
who stood pointing,
awaiting my fatal footslip.
I can hear them now
as the ambulance rushes me
to Emergency, wings akimbo:

He seemed like such a nice boy.
He was doing such a good job
fixing up the house.

Oh, yeah? Look at all this
old tar-paper on my sidewalk,
complains next-door Ike,
who leaves scrawled grievances
taped to my front door.
What was he doing up there
in the first place?
wonders down-the-street-Bev,
who studies logic at university

and likes to keep death
in its proper perspective.

I hang before them
between sea and sky,
this place I've always been.
Newborn breeze
lifts another bat wing,
blows it to the water.
Waves lick my feet.
I throw my hammer at the sun,
I raise my wings
believing I will fly.

Kim Maltman was born in Medicine Hat, Alberta, and has earned university degrees from the University of British Columbia and the University of Toronto where he teaches Physics.

OWLS

Dave Philips worked in a lab and owned a plot of land, an acre or so, he and his wife tended nights and weekends. Nothing much. Mostly just prairie grass, a little machinery, and later on a horse. One night near sunset a band in the binder snapped and sliced off the top quarter inch of one of his little fingers. For half an hour he stood there in the corner of the field, in shock, insisting that his wife keep hunting through the grass until she found it, but, it being by that time quite dark, she failed. Later a doctor dressed the finger, which soon healed. Where the tip fell to the ground the grass opened on a small patch of bare dirt. Into this dirt a bit of blood dripped. Roots, noting the moisture, pushed forth new shoots. The fingertip was chewed up by a prairie dog which was in turn swallowed by an owl. In a few days Dave Philips was back. The owl also, perched on a fence nearby, at nightfall. If you drive across the prairies in the summer you see only a pale yellow broken by clumps of grey-green sage, all dryness, and you start to think that life has a weak hold here. But you get out in the middle of it and you look closely and inside it's all green and keeps surviving. Life seethes up about you quietly. You move on, past familiar places. In a small field by the road a man looks up and waves, then turns back to the binder, having failed to recognize
your face. The cycle
continues.
The cycle
continues.

You sit there, quiet, staring out the window of the bus.
You're heading home from work again. No rain for weeks now
and the dust boils out around the wheels.
Someone, older, sits beside you, whiskers grey, his shirt
stuck to the blue vinyl, a stranger
though you know the name.
The bus is filled with them,
their shirts and dust and lunch kits, quiet breathing.
Almost everything is done now,
not much need of muscle any more this year.
Like them you want the money but you count the days down
anyway. The engine casing spews out heat
into the closed air. Dirt runs down your face.
Over the rise an elk stands by the road,
a hundred miles from anywhere.
You try to take it in. It can't survive here,
this far from the river, and you see it all at once,
this thing trapped in a place not of its own making,
barely of its own doing, and for a moment
it seems noble, almost tragic. But you're tired
and soon you start to think
that's stupid, it's an animal, they're different, and it turns its head
with a kind of frantic look as the bus passes
and the dust blows by it and the pity rises in you
so you turn your head, back into the bus,
back to the driver and the men around you, going home,
some who have come here and will come again and again and again
and to keep it from welling up inside,
you close your eyes and try to sleep a bit.

CAFES

By 9 o'clock, she thinks, she could find him if she needed to,
in one of the booths at the back of the cafe, slouched
against the wall. Maybe he'd have just come in or maybe
he'd have been there for hours already. Every so often
he'd look around as if he'd been waiting for someone who
hadn't shown up yet. Not that it matters much, there's nothing
for them to do here, weeknights, this time of year, nothing
but wait till school's over and there's work and money.
But she'd feel awkward there and out of place, so much older
than all the kids. And not that she needs to find him anyway.
Still she wishes he were coming over. She can't remember
the last time a man looked at her without making her feel ugly,
catching the eyes as they snapped away and pretended to
have been watching something else over her shoulder all the time.
She looks down at her chest. Her breasts make her angry
these days, so small, barely covering her ribs, even through the blouse.
It's the pity she hates. As if they'd earned it, most of them —
look at their bodies. She's sick of them, of teaching all the time,
of hearing their kids snicker and call her names in the schoolyard,
sick of them. Him she understands. He comes, and it's not for marks
or favors — he's already flunked 3 times and doesn't give a damn
about school — after this year he can leave anyway. He never asks for it,
he just sits there and drinks, sometimes has a cigarette,
and then takes her body when she's ready. She remembers that most of all,
the patience.

        She sits down at the kitchen table,
by the lamp, and lights a cigarette.
She knows she shouldn't smoke, it makes her nervous,
makes her hands shake, and she wishes he'd been more careful
when he came around. It's the whispers she can't stand,
the whispers and the little furtive stares. It's so easy for him,

he can just laugh back at the other kids, knowing they'd all do the same
thing if they had the chance, sex is important to them, they don't want
to be left out. But the women pretend not to understand. Some of them
were pretty once, they had nice breasts and hips, without deserving it
they could take their pick. Now that they're old and saggy
the boys just walk right by them, without looking,
even when they're lying half undressed on the lawns.
They have husbands and even though the boys are young men now
they remember husbands and it worries them —
but single women, that's different. So it serves them right,
she thinks, let them lie there, whispering to one another,
whispering and wishing it were them.

*The writing of my poetry has helped to sharpen my awareness of the
world around me and what it really is to be alive, human, and mortal.*

— *William Latta*

Dave Margoshes was born in New Jersey. He was educated at the University of Iowa and has had an international career in newspaper journalism. He came to Canada in 1972. He has published books of poetry and fiction and lives in Regina, Saskatchewan.

THE BARBER'S CHAIR

Sitting in the barber's chair
today as the razor drones
in my ear like bees whispering
secrets from the Incas
I see my father's face emerge
from beneath my beard
sudden as a bird
bursting from tangled branches
into the sieving snow.

For the smallest moment
we stare at each other,
me alive and here,
swaths of grey hair
mixed with black
in pools on my lap,
he dead a decade
but there in the mirror
just the same,
the smallest, smuggest
of smiles entwined
around the corners

of his lips,
lips that wouldn't lie
but I open my mouth
with surprise and they do.

ARITHMETIC
for Pat P.

it's arithmetic, really
and simple stuff at that
— one from two equals one —
none of this new math stuff
nothing you'd need a calculator for
just the fingers of your left hand
where the ring used to be and now
color is returning to the skin
like snow sifting in on deer tracks
or light filtering back after a shadow.

the important thing to remember
is the difference in the columns:
loss is here, on the left
gain on the right, like dark and light
the trick is all in the balance
being on a high wire
with *down* all around you, peering up —
what you need to know
isn't the weight of the loss
or the color left behind
when you peel away the one
but the feel of the gain
smooth and hard like small round stones
in the palm of your hand
and the quality of light
shining from the other.

Rhona McAdam was born in Duncan, B.C, and grew up on
Vancouver Island. She was educated at the University of Alberta
and the University of Wolverhampton, England. She now lives in
London, where she works for a human resources company. Her
books of poetry have been published in both Canada and England.

URBAN RENEWAL

The house next door is a restaurant.
We can only remember the sprawl of lawn
once played upon by children. Today
there is tarmac and the buried shards
of trees it took the men
and their bawling drills
a week to unearth and disroot.

These days all the faces we glimpse
in the windows are strangers,
intent on dinner and decor.
They do not think
to wave from the windows
and could not from this
or any distance distinguish
neighbour from thief;
we are all reduced
to transient scenery.

This is a street which turns away
from the others, where houses
pull up their springtime hedges
and wait in new green prisons,

eye each other sideways, not knowing
where the next sign will be planted.

One blooms at our gate already
and we count these final
settled days before the bricks
break apart, before the walls shake
and the old plaster cracks to show
a sawdust belly.

We enter complicity daily
by our silence, our mute
brooding over rental ads.
We are giving up this old friend
to the ones with windows in their eyes,
their steel mouths and loud hunger.
We are the last to walk here before
it becomes something else, something
new and temporary.

All down the street, houses
smooth their lawns and watch
from behind curtains,
becoming quaint and serviceable
in spite of themselves.

COUNTRY & WESTERN

A howl at the corner
of a lonesome street
it sneaks up on you
when you're lying
with your heart exposed
and it yammers at the edges
like the worst kind of pain
and it's a mouthful of everything

that rains down on you
on a winter night
so you're picking bits
of the stars out of your hair
and shaking the puddles
out of your shoes and you're missing
whoever in the wildest way
and it's the sound you always make
with your friends when you're all
belly up and down on men
and you've got that ache
that's got to be sung away.

It's a touch of twang
and a busted heart, it's the bitter
roar of 18 wheels, it's the slow
and certain clinch
of your beloved
in the arms of a stranger
or your own best friend
it's a case of everything blue
done up in fancy boots
and one hell of a wail.

HOUR OF THE PEARL

Yolanda approaches thirteen with a new haircut;
the style I don't understand but the need for it
I remember, waiting for a generation
to establish itself, give itself form.

Yolanda approaches thirteen with magic,
with subterranean lights shining from her skin.
She's finding someone new inside, building herself
layer upon layer, seeking a spirit

strong and beautiful and perfect,
holding up possibilities to the light,
finding translucence where she wants clarity.
Questions are surfacing now
that no one can answer.

Yolanda approaches thirteen with hesitation,
facing the uncertain boundaries
she must cross alone. Tonight
she fills the house with music,
sings into the ear of her friend
pressed to telephone
a few houses away; struts
into the teens
with all she has.

COMING OF AGE ON THE ISLAND

There are lights shining behind her eyes; she wakes
into a day of wing and sun, an ocean of whitecaps and sea birds.

She balances on the last step of childhood; all summer
it goes like this. She is too young, even for these men,
who come for weekends from the mainland. Around her
couples join and separate, weekend upon weekend;
she is permitted to watch like a participant.

Afternoons, she swims with her mother.
They dive in smooth waters, float on logs
caught in currents that lead to open sea.
She learns to sail, scooping wind from waves,
spells elaborate semaphore to her mother on shore.

In the evenings, the guests light fires on the beach,
roast corn, shellfish, bury bottles in the water to chill.
She drinks with them, young expert,

paddles phosphorescence when she goes to fetch beer,
fascinated by the living stars that move
beneath the surface of the water, fall from her scooped hands.

It is a summer of learning, of being put upon
for the first time. She feels the first insistence
of would-be lovers, the first shove of resistance to her refusal;
knows so much better than they that it is not her time,
not her season; her blood sings simpler melodies
than theirs. She needs nothing from them now; they let her be.

Once her mother throws a party; they chill beer
in a washtub filled with ice, buy cheese, sausage,
make party trays. Someone lights a fire. There is music.
When their guests drift into the night, joined at the hands
or waist, the daughter cleans up and goes to bed.
It is the first party she's given. It has been the night
of her first kiss, a casual buss from a middle-aged salesman
who flies in drunk on alternate weekends.

Beginnings like these become only bridges to later years.
The image of these months she will carry with her
is her mother, drifting out to sea
in their yellow life raft. Stranded herself,
she stands on the deck of a sailboat, broken mast
trailing behind her on the water, watching
as the life raft floats through the limits of her vision
carrying her mother, who is reading as she drifts
through the summer afternoon, awaiting rescue.

WHITE DRESSES

It was supposed to be romantic. It was supposed to be
an easy thing, this flight into the big world
of men and women dancing on polished floors. Instead,
of course instead, it was a parade
through the staff lounge under the eye of the headmistress,
who checked skirt lengths for decency's sake;
instead of a respite from uniform
it was the substitution of white dresses
for green tunics. On the bus, seeking the dark-eyed
lustre of glamour, we became furtive cosmeticians,
glowing whitely through the night, dextrous
with mascara and rouge by flashlight.

At the boys' school we spilled from the bus,
incandescent in the light from the gym's open door,
lurching across gravel on feet more accustomed to oxfords.
We glowed against the wall bars with sweat and rouge,
mimicking steps in the shadows, awaiting discovery
and the fearful sheen of the dance floor.

Sooner or later we were led out to the bushes
where our dresses glowed indiscreetly
and we tasted gin and cigarettes
the better to glide into the rough hands of rugby players,
press lips and braces against lips and braces,
perhaps allow small indiscretions of touch,
exchange names and grades, home towns,
then tottered back to the gym where sooner or later
the last waltz, the last grope,
the bored chaperone's beckoning hand
as the last of us were cut from the milling, suited forms
who turned pink faces and hands

up to the school bus windows, waving from the shadows
as we jerked and tumbled into the night
to fib and gossip and begin the long hope for phone calls.

DOMESTIC HAZARD

It's an elaborate system, a fine balance
of reward and punishment, rewards meted out
to suit the punishment she accepts, glass
by bitter glass, his fist curling round the clear
white heat of illness; her face burns with it
when she walks into the emergency ward
telling the old stories the nurses hear
every time she comes in: the doors she walks into
with enough force to knock out teeth; treacherous
stairwells that batter ribs, snap bones;
broom handles that leave the sign of fingers across her face,
constellations of thumb-prints on her thighs.

They shake their heads as they bandage
and splice what her home pulls apart,
press their lips together as she asks
the bitter dignity of public silence,
gathers up her children and her fear,
the weight of unacknowledged bruises,
the prospect of solitude and poverty.

She sews with the fragile thread of faith and memory
her idea of who he is, goes to save him,
accepts the dark weave of anger and illness
he throws so casually upon her; even now she's sure
there are a thousand ways she loves him,

a thousand ways he ties her heart in knots,
binds her to his side till she stifles,
no longer breathing
her own air.

MOTH LOVE

Tonight my love grows wings
and flutters around your door
with the furious energy of obsession;
tonight I find you walking outside
and tangle myself in your hair, rest on your neck
a light finger's caress, follow you
so tall, slim, fair as any candle
slip in your door in the wake
of your passage.

Tonight the white wings of my love
whisper through your sleep till you rise
to see what the noise is, cup me
helpless in your hands, step outside
fling me skyward, to where the stars
outline my desire and I wheel, dizzy
with space and cold air, descend again
to wheel, rapturous around your light
beat my wings against the hard door of refusal.

Tonight my wings are the colour of sand
and I lie in camouflage against your door
my body pressed to the pane between us.
In the morning you look outside
no memory of my presence;
in the morning you gaze unknowing
through the frosted shape of desire.

OBSCENE PHONE CALLS

They make you ask yourself
was this someone I know? Does this
disembodied voice belong
to a familiar face, someone I pass
blindly on the street, is this someone
whose elbow I've brushed in the elevator,
someone whose face I've glimpsed
beyond my window, curtained in darkness?

We learn to cut him off after the first words,
finger on the phone's button, precise
the click to silence. Calm, automatic,
hating that this must become routine,
that the daytime world disarms these calls
as if the commonplace lacks impact.
What of the fear they force of darkness
an unrecognizable voice sounding our names
over and over in the after-silence
our names caught in his mouth
how has he found our names

Our anger spreads over the city
a scattered rage that thins by morning
into vague mistrust. Every smiling face
mocks our interrupted sleep, each greeting
assumes the tones of deception
each accidental touch   is a hand that reaches
as far as the wire can go, is the obscene contact
of a stranger's mind

THE POEM

The poem keeps odd hours.
It circles itself three times before
tucking itself in for a nap, and
It won't be woken by anyone;
it has its own schedule.

In the middle of the night it yawns
from sleep. It stretches. It bounces
all over the bed until someone wakes
and when the light goes on
the poem is in the other room
waiting for someone to let it out.

It grows cantankerous if you ask it
to do something. It gives you a look
and stalks away, but it always comes back
when it's hungry.

The poem is restless if left alone.
It scratches the furniture and picks at the threads
of some part of your life you wanted
to keep perfect.

The poem doesn't care
what you want. When it wants you
it wants you, and it won't be ignored.
It leaps into your lap and sits there
until it's good and ready.

And you put up
and put up with it. And sometimes
all the thanks you get is that it leaves,
and it doesn't say when it is coming back.

You can only hope it remembers
where it came from.

ANIMAL KINGDOM

We are the intruders here
our clumsy camouflage the lodge, its logs
that dwarf the aspen, their suspicion
a muffled sibilance outside our windows.

Wilderness itches to reclaim this spot.
In the morning moths fat as fingers
cling to the window screens
another tree has fallen to the beavers
and the river bank is closer.

The mouse has sprung its trap
eaten the bait and left a single turd
in the frying pan.

Someone saw owls at daybreak
hunched in the middle of the driveway,
fixed on the lodge; owls
we cannot find
in all our books on wildlife.

AT FIFTEEN

At fifteen she is a shadow
on the horizon of her mother's sleep.

She wills the years to stop
but steps into her mother's clothes
tall as her mother's friends
and she runs.

She has found refuge
where the animals sleep
leaning against glass, where the birds
shake out wings that cannot lift them
into a sky of mirrors, where no sun
rises to mark her time.

This is her place, among the fountains
and arcades, among the endless
wardrobe of her imagination.

She swoops with her friends
and they are bright
and they are brave
and their voices rise above crowds
to wheel and echo,
trapped in the glittering dawn.

MONEY TALKS

It whispers outside her window
at night, as she lingers
between dreams that promise
the future in another part of town,
away from this world of broken
locks and basement suites.

It chatters in her ear beneath
the echoes of the mall, when she
wanders the halls, her hands
empty in her pockets or surfacing
to take the temporary warmth
of objects she'll never own.

It mutters in the voices of landlords
and teachers and grocery store clerks;

it reaches beneath her pride and bares
her life and her mother's life
and it tells them what to do.

It sneaks into her belly and growls
until she has to laugh too long
and too loud with her friends
so they won't hear what it's saying
about her.

It yells orders at her
and it takes anything it wants
and she'll spend her whole life
running toward it and
hearing it break
into laughter, just
out of reach, just
like her mother who sits today
with her hands over her ears
humming like crazy.

ANOTHER LIFE TO LIVE AT THE EDGE OF THE
YOUNG AND RESTLESS DAYS OF OUR LIVES

I am not going to get maudlin about this
but it seems like everything happens to me
and there's nothing I can do but go along
with it.
        What else can you do, this is life
and if it means you get amnesia or split
personalities or one of those unmentionable
female disorders or your husband gets trapped
in a south american mine shaft and you don't know
if he's alive or dead and you remarry
only this time your man's displaced nobility

who turns out to be your long lost cousin so
the priest says you have to separate and he
 disappears in a plane crash but turns up again
years later looking entirely different
and marries your best friend who's told she's
terminally ill so she lies on a *chaise longue*
for many months while around you
both there are things going very wrong
only very slowly so you spend days on the same
conversation changing clothes every time
you leave the room,
                                        well so be it.

It's not that I'm complaining,
or, heaven help me, having another nervous breakdown,
but I feel sometimes that everything happens
to me.
                        I felt it just last month when I was
vacationing in Acapulco and who should check in
next door but my first husband who'd been
trapped in a south american mine shaft and no one
knew if he was alive or dead, and here he is
looking somewhat the worse for wear but perfectly
okay except that he'd taken up with some bad
company and was smuggling cocaine into Florida
but later I found out it was against his will
because he was being blackmailed by some modern
day pirates who'd discovered his real identity
after he'd disgraced himself with a Mexican barmaid
after they'd drugged him and set up a video camera
and were threatening to send a tape to the newspaper
in our town which would have just ruined his
plans of coming back and running for senator
not to mention the hurt it would have caused
his family, who have quite a good name, really,
though there's been just a hint of madness in

most of them, including me but they sent me
to quite an exclusive little clinic in the mountains
for a season and now I'm right as rain, which
is something considering I was having an affair
with my psychiatrist who turns out to be an old
classmate of my husband's, the one who was trapped
in the mine shaft in south america at the time, though
at this stage here he is right next door in the
same resort in Acapulco, and he sneaks over at night
and confesses what he's been up to for the last
six seasons, and I tell him how his son is all
grown up and running a model agency right there
in the old home town, and we get quite emotional
and decide to forgive and forget and so I call
the police but before they come the bad guys
catch us together and tie me up and leave me
in the boat-house with the tide coming in and I
look like a goner but my husband, the one
from the mine shaft, is able to cut his ropes
free with an emery board I slipped him and he
knocks out his captors and with the police on his heels
he finds me just in time, my hair's hardly wet,
and they save me and we get to come back to our
old home town and have a lovely wedding with
my best friend as my maid of honour, though
by this time she's pretty weak, and after we
leave on our honeymoon she just fades away, there
on the patio with rose blossoms falling on her head
and my bouquet falling from her hand as the music
swells and the titles come up and the season ends.

COAT OF MANY POEMS

She has hung him
round with lovely words,
made him
an admirable piece of work.

He doesn't need to say
anything. She is not even sure
if he is still there
beneath the weight
of decoration.

She listens
but hears nothing.
He has made tracks
beyond the reach of artifice.
He is doing fine
without rhyme and image and she
has his beautiful shell.

*The poet captures a physical landscape and, underlying this, an emotional
landscape in the same frame. Successful poems are those in which readers
not only see something familiar in the physical depiction but also recognize
something of themselves in the emotional dimension.*

— *Greg Simison*

Colin Morton was born in Toronto and grew up in Calgary. He was educated at the University of Calgary and the University of Alberta. He has had a career as a teacher, editor, researcher, poet and fiction writer. He now lives in Ottawa.

PICKLED WATERMELON

pocket knife's best
but even a fingernail will do

keep the hole small, scrape out the pulp
till the cork fits snug
then carefully, repeat
carefully pour

lick any spills off the fat green flank —
go ahead, spill a bit,
that's the best part

once I poured three bottles of rum
into one of these babies

mind you it was really juiced
we were licking booze off each others' arms —
come to think of it that's the best part

but one bottle is plenty
to sweeten your weekend

just cool her overnight
while she sucks up the juice

and the lake will be brighter than ever tomorrow —
the sun will be red
juicy red

time was
we had no fridge at the lake

left the melon instead
over night in the spring fed stream —
and really that's best

but one summer
we left one in the shallows
fat and pickled

next morning she was gone
no sign

all Saturday we steamed
did you take her? then who?

till we found
on the path to the privy
a raccoon

black eyes glassy
crazy grin on its face
and stiff

MY FATHER WRITES A POEM HOME FROM
EUROPE ON HIS PARENTS' SILVER ANNIVERSARY, 1945

> *war*
> *knees*
> *far*
> *cease*

the rhymes don't matter now

but I wonder where and
who he was
the day he took out
the ON ACTIVE SERVICE paper
> (in York awaiting orders?
> or a smouldering Dutch village?
> on one of those long drugged days
> in a French hospital?)
to write what he would never say

> *Fight for home and you*

is that what he meant by the wounded look
that is all I saw my father give
his father while he lived?

weddings *claim* children
as a sniper claims victims
and when I read

> *A Heritage which soldiers bought*
> *For every girl and boy*

I break out in a sweat
see spots and get the shits

in short   it's a soldier's life
being the son of a soldier

> I am so glad
> this was my father's only poem
> glad he didn't teach me
> to marry or give birth to war

> if it left him nothing to teach
> all right
> I've learned more from his silence
> than I could from all
> the poems he never wrote

PATCHING

> week on week I patch
> and go on patching fabric
> that no longer holds a thread
>
> patch night on day then
> pick loose ends and
> go on patching
>
> when you arrive you
> might see me
> all in one piece
> but soon
> I begin picking
> pulling
> before your eyes
> I fray
>
> only later in bed or
> on the floor
> I see

the cloth I needle
is my flesh

SPRING SNOW

haiku are snowing
gently over
cars in the parking lot
between the red brick
wings of the hospital

snowflakes large as
scraps of torn paper
haiku written on them
almost legible
on the darkening sky

we are waiting together
as you've been waiting
nine months now
the cat on your lap

slowly pushed down from
your stomach to your knees
by the hidden stranger
learning to swim
inside you

tonight our waiting
is almost over
and outside the window
it's snowing haiku

that muffle the sound
of traffic
of the icebound
river breaking open

EMPTY BOTTLES

line up all the empty bottles

the long-necked beer bottles from the antique store

the wine bottles and pop bottles left on beaches

steam off the labels and line the bottles up, the green
    ones with the brown black yellow and clear ones

line up the beer bottles whose labels have been torn off
    by neurotic fingers

and the bottles sent back to the breweries because they
    have cockroaches or dead mice at the bottom

line up the bottles afloat on all the seas, those with
    messages in them and those without any

and the bottles with methyl-hydrate-soaked cotton in
    them used by schoolkids for killing insects

line up the bottle that killed Malcolm Lowry with the
    bottle that killed Dylan Thomas and the bottles
    that killed all the drunken poets nobody's heard
    of and the poets who spoke all their lines into
    their bottles

and all of Purdy's crocuses that weren't smashed on the
    sides of frozen roads when thrown from car windows

line up the bottles of dark glass we look through darkly
    when we want to see the ghosts of our former selves

and the bottles Dr. Jekyll drank from, and all the Dr. Jekylls
    whether on the stage in movies or on television

and the bottles of rubbing alcohol and aftershave and
    nail-polish remover people only drink from in
    dark alleys

line up the embalming fluid bottles someone was saving
    to build a glass house some day

and the bottles of nerve gas saved up for the war nobody
    wants

and the bottles of toxic gas cruising the streets disguised
    as trucks

and the pill bottles, the billions of pill bottles
    emptied every year, and the billions that sit
    half-empty for years on medicine shelves

line up the empty bottles sent back by the hospitals
    for refills

line up all the empty bottles

the party's over

Brenda Niskala was born in Outlook, Saskatchewan and raised on a farm in an area known as Big Valley. She is a graduate of the University of Saskatchewan and currently works as an administrative executive in the literary arts. She lives in Regina.

PRAIRIE JUNK

vines twist through wheels
of rusted implements   here horses   the old
power sources graze   long-hooved   kick
cracking leather straps
where pitchforks stab the air
near dust-filled gunny sacks
stovepipes shelter scurrying
things that form tangled nests
in limp barbed wire   birds
like dry insects   ghost
in old barn yard

I WILL NOT BE THE GRANDMOTHER

I will not be the grandmother
who tickles children's feet
tucks feather quilts
around tiny sticky-sweet chins
who winks   lifting the top from the candy dish

my hands tight on green snakes
mouth full of bitter cherry juice
I'll prepare my grandchildren for the fight
with hard words   dry bone arms
I'll love them fiercely

Charles Noble was born in Lethbridge, Alberta. He is a graduate of the University of Alberta. He works the ancestral farm near the village of Nobleford, Alberta. He is a grain farmer with a passion for philosophy and since 1972 has been publishing books of poetry.

HORSE AROUND

My father built an airplane,
then pushed off the roof with it,
no damage.

Wired the outhouse, wrong man,
electrified his father.

Built a cannon, splintered
the chicken coop.

Put a gopher and a lantern
in a huge box kite,
flew them at night
preparatory to God knows what
or maybe settled-for bridge-*out*
empathy.

Interrupted a dining room meal
with a crystal set in the basement
setting off a bomb in the yard
that rained heavy dirt on the roof.

Sprinkled feed in the garden
for the chickens,
blasted the heck
out of their pecking order.

His father had six hundred work horses,
all he wanted
was a bicycle, probably armored.

By the time I came along
technology had been wrested
out of the avant-garde,
peace ushered in.

I went straight
for the first gentle horse.

THE WAY THE MIND WORKS

Five sixty-five the Chinese take-out food
comes to,
busy mind thinks a five and then a one
to cover, busier mind
thinks sixty-five is chewing
its oneness caught
out by the notch, the gnaw in a knowledge over
the edge of a ledger-
demain, chow mein noodles' doodles'
dot, puts down another one put down
to the indentured dot forever
indenting the blotch on its selfish
lessness, like the diminishing dust to
the backed-up panning swallowing swallowing
its guilty swallow, repast in the present box

Chinese
man looking up as he touched his glasses popped
open the cash register,
dipped his hand into cubed chicken
and vegetables with pineapple sauce.

He made a suggestion
and since I was hungry
I took him up on it.

As I was eating I felt dizzy
like I was falling out of an airplane.

When I finished
he said I "ate the float".

In the way that the Holy Grail myth was about the quest rather than the goal, I think that poetry is more about process than product. I suppose I'm less interested in the question of what makes a writer decide to stop tinkering with a given piece than I am in the question of when the poem itself ends.

—Jay Ruzesky

Peter Ormshaw was born in Regina, Saskatchewan, and has earned degrees from Queen's University and Cambridge University. He is a member of the RCMP in an Alberta detachment.

PICKING UP MOM

It was just after football practice, I remember that
because my hair was wet from the shower
and my muscles were light but still full of blood
making me walk in an easy, broad way.

Dad's busy at home grouting
around the bathtub so he sends me out
to get my mother at her appointment, pick her up
at the main entrance at the Civic.
His hands liver-spotted with silicone
thumb and forefinger pluck keys from a pocket
toss them at me.
I'm young, enough
to catch without looking, always knowing
where everything is, just able to grab it.

My hair is long and wind
fingers it through the window. I'm not worried
about catching a cold, the day is warm
like mid-July, though September is nearly done.
I drive too fast behind the powerful engine
of my father's car, but I drive
with the road and not against it,
leave the driveway with the first chords
of Supertramp on the radio

arrive at the hospital doors just as Bruce Springsteen
finishes *Born to Run*, perfectly orchestrated.

But she's not waiting, doesn't appear
after a few more minutes, honk of the horn
so I ignore the loading zone signs and park.

It's a new building, all efficiency on the outside
marble inside and white to make it Roman.
When wide sliding doors move aside I can't see her
at first, but there she is behind a clot of white coats
half-behind a pillar and I walk to her
jangling the keys around my finger expecting
her to see me. She sees me
but doesn't spring up, stays leaned against the pillar
and starts to weep, quiet at first, then I hear her. I run
and because I never hold her
this is the first time I understand the way her head meets me
at my chest when we stand toe-to-toe.

I don't want to know so I ask fast,
what's wrong what's wrong but she can't get it out
through shudders so I hold her tighter
till she says *it's the X-rays.*
What X-rays? I answer, she says
to get the X-rays or picture of something
they made her drink orange juice, quarts and quarts
and now she can't stand up without diarrhea.
Diarrhea I say, she nods, sucks tears off her top lip.
I say it again and again to be sure and as I say it I'm already laughing
and her feet are lifted off the ground. We're
walking towards the sliding doors seconds later
and she's yelling at me to put her down
but she's so light,
my heart is so light.

COUGARS
for the Ottawa-Carleton regional champions, 1979

Sweat from the grass playing fields
rises fragrant with frost, wet
earth and rot of rusted leaves.

Football season smell. Snap crackle
tinge in the nose, in the bones
a yearning for contact. Pop
of impact, head-to-head drills
then ooze of shower drooled heat,
Mentholatum deep.

Distant in our suburb
we had sub-lives, cozy
within leather team jackets,
protected by shoulder pads.
Heaven was a just heaven, blue sky
with cirrus cloud stripes —
a referee's sweater.

Sky is held breath before kick-off.

That was the season we didn't lose,
nothing touched us all year
except for the breeze, empathetic dance
of Black Watch skirts and perfume
of mist above the white-lined fields,
just before dusk, before winter.

SHOES

A pair of baby shoes
constructed with hide,
waxed thread, nails.

Stiff for lack of wear
these were recovered
from a storehouse
glutted with tongues,
laces and soles.

This final exhibit
at Yad Vashem
reduces six million
to a pair of feet.

Let them say
this number
is exaggerated.

Poetry arises from events, real or imagined, that stir the intellect and emotions to recreate, through words, the full impact of life's greatest challenges.

— Lesley Choyce

Don Polson was born in New Brunswick, raised in Oshawa, and lived in Windsor, Ontario until his death in 1989. He was educated at Queens University and Wayne State. He had a career in psychiatric social work.

HE DIES TO SPEAK THE TRUTH

" . . . we were powerless over alcohol . . .
our lives had become unmanageable."
                    Alcoholics Anonymous

His eyes are filled with honest pain
as he dies to speak the truth:

"Twice now I've screwed things up
because of it. The first time in a blackout.
Came to the next morning.
Blood on the bedroom floor. The mirror
smashed to hell. A note left on
the kitchen table saying 'It can't go on
this way'. I shook the whole mess off,
stayed clean awhile, but soon it was
as bad as ever. Next time was in
some classy bar and blood again.
The cops' and mine. See?
Here's the scar to prove it. Did six weeks
in the slammer. Just out last Tuesday
morning. I've hardly touched a drop
since then — I'm stronger. It's different now.
Jesus, I know it's going to be."

AN APRIL LYRIC

Carefully lowered
into the soil and cut
from its burlap casing,
the mountain ash,
brought home earlier
this torrid April day,
stands slim and quivering
in the fading light
— a childlike thing
in strange surroundings.

Too frail to bear
the trust of curious squirrels
or even small finches,
it's left in its humility
to wait awhile
for strength that earth
and sun engender
— my part is done.

Alone with it a moment,
I sense a little of
the origin of prayer
and dream a flowering
of the empty space around
— my eyes already
eager to consume
the turning leaves,
the red-gold berry cluster
of a cooler season.

AUTUMN RHYME

At evening now the stars glow softer
over dancing trees,
the measured screech of insects muffled
by a rising breeze.
Dreading this time, while then carousing
with the wanton sun,
I bask in these shadowy hours; mock
the green-flamed summer gone.
Still, drifting leaves and fallen petals
poison all-knowing smiles;
sometimes harsh distances I would accept
for gentler downhill miles.

DECEMBER TWILIGHT

Evening dims over the dark orchard.
The trees, arthritic and worn from
their autumnal labour, moan stiffly
in the wind. I have come here for no
good reason, have sought no benediction.
But suddenly, low on the horizon, a last full
shaft of light bursts from beneath the clouds.
It sings across the fields of golden snow.
Attentive, I hear the trees anew,
their sounds turned to the murmur of
a supplicant's response. How good to feel

such sounds becoming too my whispered
gratitude which will sustain throughout
these death-mocked solstice days.

*The word and the image are to poetry what character and scene are to
narrative.*

—*Lewis Horne*

Garry Radison was born in Kamsack, Saskatchewan. He is a graduate of the University of Regina. He teaches English and Drama in Yorkton, Saskatchewan where he lives. His first book of poetry was published in 1978.

ALL THERE IS
for Shelley

Dust covers the town
after every breathing.

The hidden dying of strangers
is unreasonable, leaving nothing

as if our lives could be saved up
and stuffed in the mouth on cue.

The town you return to
is an illusion

propped up on the prairie
the night before you appear.

One does not inhabit but is inhabited.
Dry grass and a stuttering wind.

All there is to come to,
that can be revealed.

All that you must hear,
and hear it for it is my sound too,

whispering grass, night wind stirring,
whatever can be discovered and said.

Monty Reid was born in Spalding, Saskatchewan. He is a graduate of the University of Alberta and currently works at the Tyrell Museum in Drumheller, Alberta. He has been publishing books of poetry since 1979 and is also an essayist and fiction writer.

SKIDOOERS

The big jack stretches and unstretches
toward the fence, the movement of a heart
contract, expand, floating across
the snow.

Six of us: two Kawasakis, two Yammies,
one John Deere, one old SkiRoule with
high loops welded onto the front of the skis
so he can go over the wire.

The jack breaks for the scrub
angling off for the fenceline and we
swing in behind him, thighs sore against
the machine's push, trying to intersect
the jack's line to the fence.

But he can run.
We pull up beside, the black eyes not moving
the legs bunching, thrusting, but he's too
close to the fence and we can't cut him off.

So we pull up, except for Stan
on one of the big Yamahas, riding in close
to the rabbit and trying to stare him down
and hit the fence at it must have been
close to fifty.

One strand slicing through the fibreglass
cowling and then snapping, the other rides
up over the windscreen, catching Stan across the armpits
one barb hooked into the nylon suit
standing up because the sudden stopping was lifting
him up and forwards and the wire takes him
across the chest, whipping him off the machine
backwards into the snow.

And the jack running and the machine running
the throttle jammed open
and Stan lying in the snow
a spot of blood under his nose.

THE DISPOSAL OF HAZARDOUS WASTES

The cultivator unfolds the earth: old
letters. We read them again and again.
The shovels turn the worms up and they lie
like veins on the surface, stunned by light.
Dirt runs through them like blood.
When they move the birds get them,
pluck them in their beaks like string.

Here in the yard a nest of mouths
they stitch together. They stand
on the lip of twigs and dangle the worms.
Drop them, preen, and are gone.
They feed all day. The next they
follow the sprayer across the second
quarter, its booms spread out
for balance: tightrope
of earth.

The air takes the spray apart
and even though there is no wind

we can smell it. It hangs
in the yard like the must
of old papers bound with twine
and stacked in the basement.
What is it we write
to ourselves?

The day after, we found the gawky
bodies on the lawn. Plucked out,
veins blue with pesticide, transparent
skin. We picked them up and
threw them in the ditch. A cat
will probably find them. And as we
walked from the house to wherever
we could hear the birds, their songs
tumble over and over
out of the air.

THE CROTCHETY OLD LADIES PLAY SCRABBLE

They drink tea and eat
thin wafers and their dresses
are discreetly long. They draw
letters, arrange them into words
tag one word to another. The game
fits them like an old nightie.
Compulsion. I get such lousy
letters Ida says and every word
I make is just the one you need.
Her patience frays. Molly
is the other one. She's played
for years and has a long string
of victories but long strings end.
Says Ida. A dictionary is by her hand.
She makes up her own rules.

Double letter, triple word, they
kill the afternoon with names.
There is no end to remembering.
If I could only get my letters out
they say. The tea goes bitter
at the end.

I am in awe of the power of poetry to move. Of all the genres, poetry is the one that most engages our subconscious, presents the mystery of the soul in its most concisely rendered form.

—*Eva Tihanyi*

Ken Rivard was born in Montreal and lives in Calgary. He writes poetry, fiction and children's stories. He has published four books, and has had his work anthologized and published in numerous collections and magazines.

HUMPBACKS IN THE SKY

in the early evening whales slip
across the sky leaving sunset coals to smolder
like fingers poking at black land.

whales absorb the day's heat
from a copper lake
ignoring the creators
like a faceless photographer
in a crowd.

man who took this picture
rides on mammals' backs
saddled on the quiet of tomorrow.

as the earth squeezes those last sky drops
into its breast
whales glide to a place
where picture-takers
and sky-creatures prepare
the broken day.

VARIABLES OF MY FATHER'S AMBITION

as he legs his way into the house
necktie is loosened, jacket is flung
like leftover skins from his day.
a carefully folded newspaper is tossed
onto the living-room rug in unison with his:
what's for supper, Ethel?
as if the moon were asking the sky
for its latest menu of thunderheads.

when we eat supper, he dons his comic faces
by mocking his co-workers —
their functions are beyond their control.
he doesn't even know he's doing it
as I choke from another of his custard pies
on my face.

at night when everybody is smiling in their sleep
he wakes me for a Marx Brothers movie.
I sit on the floor between his ankles
waiting for that starting gun of laughter.

his convulsions explode from my ears
to my shoulders
to my belly
and before I know it
my father and I are one loud honk
chasing skirts around the television.

during a commercial, I see my father on a studio lot
teaching The Marx Brothers how to be funny.
the way he clarifies
yes, the way he clarifies Harpo's philosophy of bum-pinching.

when the lesson is over my father is presented
with an Academy Award — best ability for comic instruction
and The Marx Brothers promise to do their next film with him.
right away he calls me up to the stage
gives me his award with such a hilarious look
it causes all the Oscars to step down
and applaud his performance.
even the audience files up to him
like ripples of laughter dressed just right.
the only hereness left
in the widest grin of chairs imaginable
and the endless
hopes of my father.

RELIEVER

he strolls in from centre field.
his turn to relieve.
a man in the crowd points
to the pitcher's mound
flings out advice
but the pitcher's glove catches and quietly
drops the spectator's advice on the turf.
the man, still gesturing, reminds the reliever:
keep your fastball low
don't let your curve hang
be sure your slider ...
and the crowd gulps down
the man and his words.

reliever trudges to the mound slowing down
as his plan picks up tempo.

he looks up at the man
pretends to nod
warms up by tossing back at his father
those two words still caught
in the webbing of his glove.

ICE TIME

cutting across a park in late November
I stop,
hear voices coming from the bottom
of an empty swimming pool.
a group of boys are playing hockey
with the yellow of a tennis ball.
I don't disturb them.
imagine, playing ball hockey
on the floor of an autumn pool.
the boys are warming up
taking shots from the shallow end
to the deep end.
goaltender finds it easier that way
and
he is using school bags for goalposts.
now that makes sense.
he is letting his friends learn
to put homework
where it should be,
in the middle
of an almost November dark.

Inspiration is all around: in whispers, tornadoes, egg rolls, umbrellas,
yellow knapsacks and red birthday bikes. I watch, listen, experience.

— *Shelley A. Leedahl*

Jay Ruzesky was born in Edmonton and educated at the University of Victoria and the University of Windsor. He lives in Victoria, B.C., and teaches at Malaspina College.

MY GRANDFATHER WAS OFFERED A CONTRACT WITH THE DODGERS BUT MY GRANDFATHER'S FATHER OFFERED HIM THE FARM AND SAID HE COULDN'T HAVE BOTH

Unless you want it to, it rains.

Long drive in the back seat,
landscape yawns,
baked fields out either window
and funnels of precious earth rising.
Cumulonimbus.

He is a very old farmer.
You are very young, not yet labelled
by anything you do. You pull away from Nanton,
the nursing home fades
like a baseball player in right field.

You are always on the losing team.
During a game he leans behind the backstop
the only time you ever throw
from the outfield all the way to home plate.
A magnet,
the ball like steel attracted to him. *Out.*
You see him there, a static
image of his contentment,
a culmination of something: time past.
Up six-five the penultimate inning,

it rains.
Later, you lose the rematch.

The phone rings. You've never seen your mother
cry like that before.
Holds you for something to ground herself.

After the funeral you crouch
in the backyard trying to invent grief.
They have given you an old glove that was his.
He could have been in the big leagues
but had to choose.
You trace a finger across the cracked leather palm,
straining for sadness.
You hardly knew him but want misery,
water on the earth. You want,
like everyone else,
loss and requiem — the long toss to home.

LEARNING TO SMOKE

Life is so short that history
might repeat itself: your mother
behind the barn in the forties. Smoke
of the dandelion stem curling
sickly sweet between her and
your future uncle, her sister too
leaning against a red tractor wheel,
buzzing with the puff.

Your first smoke behind the summer
hockey rink, Labatt's cans like chaotic pucks
where ice was, three of you,
a green pack of Export shit-ends
from a carton on the fridge.
What were you doing out so long,

hesitating while the streetlights
came on? You rush in
to wash and brush.
And later,   the year
the teachers go on strike
you discover grass,
small soapstone pipes to smoke it in.
You watch *The Flintstones* like
never before, do your best
to hide your breath, red eyes,
try not to buzz,
talk evasively to your mother,
as if she doesn't know.

THE ONE RIGHT GIRL IN THE WORLD FOR YOU
ON THE STREETCAR GOING BY

Your conscientious eyes dart around

                                                in the library,
at the grocery,

                        at bus stops
and on streetcars.

You look at reflections downtown in the
mirror glass of the Bank of Montreal building,
check skating rinks, cafes, and you ride
the Bloor line to the edge of morning
thinking about the girl in grade four
who used to punch you hard in the arm
when Ms. Chase turned around; the one time
you hit her back you were sent to see Mr. May
in the office and he leather-strapped you,
five good ones across the palm saying
'You should never, ever, ever, ever,
never, ever hit a girl.'

In the Dupont subway station
you remember your first kiss:
Kurt coming at you with mistletoe
and Janet at the John Ware Junior
High School dance, adolescent bodies
practising epileptic fits against
the assassinated music of a local garage band.
Your breath mouth lips fit together
for a microsecond, that first taste.
You didn't brush your teeth until
the following afternoon, but she
moved away before the second semester
and was absent the day of the class picture —
gone without saying

                              goodbye.

Summer sneaks in like a bit of bad advice
drawing gibbous moons under your armpits.

You wait at crosswalks downtown trying to
peek in the back seats of taxis going by.
You sit on benches.

Always, your pocket full of change.

THE COMPLETE POEMS OF MR. JOHN MILTON

My car and I were down on Oak
just past seventy-first before the bridge,
hood up, CAA called, waiting with people
squealing by as though my breakdown was planned
for their inconvenience though the bus drivers
and street cleaner seemed sympathetic in their
paid-by-the-hour way as they paused to slip around me
into the next lane like cogs engaging a fast-turning
gear, and at one point I got out and looked

under the hood at the wires and bolts and hoses
and all those *things* that have purpose
and I poked around because the
people in the house whose phone I had
used were watching and I didn't want to
let on I didn't know what I was doing, then
I hooked my shirt on a metal edge
and stood up fast ripping it open
so I decided to just sweat it out
so I wiped my brow and rubbed my eyes
(a mistake because of the grease);
I took the shirt off and got back
in the car to wait and there was a book
of Milton's poetry on the passenger
seat and since I hadn't read *Paradise Lost*
I started reading, aloud, which is how
I was told Milton is best appreciated and
I'd just started the part about Satan cast "to
bottomless perdition, there to dwell
in Adamantine Chains and penal fire"
when the CAA mechanic rapped on my window
and I looked back at him and

said *am I glad to see you*

WE TAKE PHOTOGRAPHS

Doing my best James Dean down the boulevard.
Shoulders hunched,
cigarette tucked in the corner of my mouth,
collar up, hands in the pockets of the great,
long coat, wrinkle
in my brow.
Walking through drizzle.

We photograph ourselves
in mirrors; invent image privately.
Expecting *Rebel Without a Cause,*
I catch myself
between two naked mannequins
in a department store window,
zipper wide open.
Click.

If Shakespeare were alive today, he would be finding metaphors for his love poems in such developments as e-mail. In fact, he'd be sending his poems out over the Internet.

— Bert Almon

Barbara Sapergia was born in Moose Jaw, Saskatchewan. She was educated at the University of Saskatchewan and the University of Manitoba. She was a founding member of Thunder Creek Co-op and continues to be involved with literary publishing. Sapergia lives in Saskatoon and writes poetry, fiction, and drama for stage, radio, television, and film.

FIREDANCE

sharpening my pencil for the fifth time
looking idly out the window to the northwest
i see them meeting in a flash of flame
& skyshapes too low, too large

this timing could not have been rehearsed
though many here have trained for it
orange Harvards buzzing down corridors of air
back & forth over the city

in one perfect instant
like the planet Mars seeking conjunction
one of them is drawn to the North Star
hurtling through the air

at recess we pour from the school
& flock to the northern gate, waiting
until the side door opens
& the grade 8 boys march out
with the relentless grace of a trained army
they don't look at us children
their eyes fixed only on the gate
no one stops them

afterwards they drift home
faces like ashes & pale sand
for an instant I see inside my brother's skull
pictures of broken bodies, their limbs
scattered to the earth & wind
flung down beside or fused to
bits of bright silver metal

all across the city
boys sit at the table but cannot eat
much later my brother speaks
we didn't know

COTEAU

from Tombstone Hill
Old Wives Lake shimmers under pounding sun
i think of the Bible & the Dead Sea
but i stand in a circle of stones

in this country
you are never alone
wind always with you
even rocks alive
with rust & gold lichens
in the sun
warm rock yields

a hawk hangs on a curve of air
searching for meat
& not to please my eye
in the coulee wolf willow flares silver
these hills feel old, brown backs
like sleeping buffalo
big as hills

i lie on rock
feel the throb
of ten thousand hooves
drum against grass
against warm & yielding earth

in this country
you are never alone
wind all around you
& the piercing odour
of sage rubbed in the hand
hot sky skimming the land
long grass dancing

Stephen Scriver grew up in Wolseley, Saskatchewan, and gradu-
ated from the University of Saskatchewan. He has been a school-
teacher and has a long career of coaching track, football and hockey,
and has gained national recognition for his hockey poems. He lives
in Edmonton.

THE SLAP SHOT
for Rudy Wiebe

   You see, the problem is:

   to get your head above and
just ahead of the puck

   to slide your forehand down
the shaft of your stick as you
pull it back

   and with your back leg leaving
the ice just before your stick hits

   striking the ice just a few
inches behind the puck

   hitting it about the middle
of the blade

   while aiming at a corner of
the net

and if you have to think about
   that, brother

   it just isn't there

ICARUS

"*Get in there, Wagner,*
    and get that damn puck!"

He's over the boards
in flight
into cold, escapeless sky

the palsied cries below
dissolve into a roar

his mortal fears are
masked by insolence

as he wings at the disc
and the beer's golden
glare of the sun

Poetry works best when it assumes a dynamic relationship between the writer and the reader or listener.

— Lyle Weis

Greg Simison was born in Guildford, England. He attended the University of Calgary and currently lives in Vernon, B.C. He is a poet and playwright.

MY FAMILY'S UNDER CONTRACT TO CANCER

every few years,
renewing its option,
it claims another aunt, uncle, cousin
relegating our infrequent gatherings
to the level of witch hunts:
eyes probing chests
for evidence of disguised mastectomies,
the hoarse throat of a lingering cold
solid proof
of its black progress through vocal chords
and God pity the poor fool who,
inhaling carelessly,
breaks into a coughing fit . . .
condemned for the rest of the evening
to know that
behind every affectionate smile,
every tender handclasp,
he's watching another name
scratched from the Christmas list,
another reunion table
minus one more chair.

FALLING IN LOVE

how appropriate the term is
with its implication of a loss of balance

in the highwire act of the emotions
the potentially fatal flaw

TRAVESTY

from 300 feet
wings suddenly retracted
the osprey plunges to the lake
emerging
seconds later
with a fish any of us would envy

half a mile away
crouched in this ridiculous boat
I ruefully scan
my lightweight German casting reel
the 'never sink' tackle box
crammed with a hundred bucks
in 'sure fire' lures
and desperately trying to ignore
old Mother Nature's pro
showing me up
with a set of claws
that
were it feasible
any half-assed department store
could duplicate and market
at 59 cents apiece

WEST OF OLDS

standing before the grave
of a grandfather I never knew
I recall the family legend;
how he'd nearly died in the Halifax explosion
how
pulled from the water
he lay piled with the dead for 6 hours
before someone noticed movement
only to die
some 15 years later
from the deteriorating effect of his wounds

and I can understand
why he chose this particular spot
this quiet backwater
tucked between the wheat and the mountains
a thousand miles from the nearest sea
and the disturbing roar of colliding ships

Glen Sorestad was born in Vancouver, B.C., but has spent most of his life in Saskatchewan. He had a long career as an English teacher and was a founding member of the Saskatchewan Writers' Guild and Thistledown Press. He has been publishing books of poetry since 1973. He lives in Saskatoon.

AIDE MÉMOIRE

The world begins and ends in memory;
what I remember is what I am.

Did that blade of grass I plucked
as a boy to vibrate with my breath

really burst the air with shrillness?
A remembered world holds truth

and realities far clearer than echoes.
In the cupped hands of remembrance

the thin green reed of what we are
trembles with a sound so rare.

CAT IN MORNING

See how the distant
ages live
       in this
              soft tread
      this slow,
                deliberate
stalk;

                how many savage
kills
        ripple
                its sleek fur.
This cat lives
                on death.
Forget
        the lazy afternoon
comfort
        in its throaty
                        purr.
The breast-torn
                        bird
knows nothing
                of this sound.
It is morning
                now and
its careful
                step
                        worries
the small
        of fur
                and feather.
The cat
        is stealth
moving
        through time,
its blood
        hot,
its belly
        empty.

FOURTEEN

Whatever became of blue-eyed Jeannie
whose swelling breasts were magnetic fields
that seized our eyes like iron filings?

In our coltish play of bump and push
we teased and ran from discovery's edge,
ran like scolded pups from her mock-chiding.

That summer's sudden rounding of her body
caught us unprepared at fall's return;
the thrust of her newness thundered,
rolled our boyhood summers into the past,
triggered a new volcanic surge
that drove our nights to wonder.

TWO FISH, ONE MORNING

Late October, a cold morning,
we were driving home to the farm
from the city for the weekend:
Why do I remember this now?
Why now, with you gone, the memory
like an empty place at a family dinner?

"Let's stop at the lake and fish,"
you said; I argued for a warm bed.
But you persisted,
you often did, and we stopped there —
the pre-dawn chill, deserted shoreline,
the boats of summer now high and dry,
but for one; and we rowed out on the grey
slight chop as dawn shivered

with autumn frost. Offshore we anchored,
fumbled numb-fingered over tackle,
our backs hunched against the cold breeze.

All of this was thirty years ago:
two brothers, a whim you had that I
acceded to as brothers do. Remember
how the grey sky lightened
and the wind grew, made us huddle
on the floor of that old wooden rowboat,
our clothes unsuited to this wild notion?

We cast our chosen lures and cursed
our numb and gloveless hands
that didn't want to be here at all.
Then the first pike hit your lure so hard
it snapped you upright, almost pitched
you overboard; and you fought the fish
until it pounded on the floor beside us —
twelve pounds of fury, its sleek skin
curiously warm to my stiffened fingers.

Soon I too was fighting one, its sudden
strike setting my cold hands to work
as if fisherman's memory was energy
to fuel numb hands with fire. I too
reeled the large and vicious pike
(it could have been a deadringer for yours)
to the boat and you reached into the chill
water, hauled the fish in by the leader.

And we leaned against the sides,
kindled with excitement and laughter,
and stared at the two largest pike
we'd ever taken from these waters.
We fished no more that morning.

Nor ever again. It was the last time
we fished together, though I have since
dreamed many trips we should have taken,
as our lives pulled us separate ways.

But now, this sudden retrieval, this double
barb of memory: that day, when for a time
we were as one — a single fisherman,
hooked, sinew and bone, to a single fish —
one cold morning in October when
for a time there was no time at all
and we were either nothing or everything,
two brothers crazed with the wisdom of fools.

THE AMATEUR GARDENER

The salmon-fleshed begonias have wilted
and died from over-watering, drowned.

Just yesterday he was certain that he
heard them crying out for water.

Their once-proud sockeye blooms are now
a mere soggy memory. To kill with kindness,

he reflects, is every bit as certain as rage,
as he dumps the drowned begonia in the garbage.

Even now he thinks he hears the fern croak
dustily from its pot. He stops his ears.

TUNNELS

When they entered the darkness
their headlights were futile gestures.

He was several years into his eighties
and she a few years younger. Tunnels

through mountains were an unknown terror
they broached on faith alone. His eyes,

enfeebled by age, books and grain dust
could not adjust to the absence of light;

her voice guided his hands on the wheel,
led them from day through night to day.

In his eighty-fifth year he crumpled
with a stroke that left his memory

a highway grid fraught with tunnels
on every road. Now in the nursing home

she talks with him each day, her voice
his eyes still, still the guide that steers

him through the past, through memories
she had not even shared. His hands still

cling to the steering wheel as she speaks,
as she leads them surely down the road.

They are both driving through the dark;
moving surely to a brilliance of light.

FACES

I only know you
as you are now

not the young woman
who turned men's heads
made their blood leap
like a vaulting deer

You smashed
through the car's windshield
your face
a sudden frightened explosion
of glass shards

They wheeled you to the surgeons
masked in bandages
built you a new face
made you another woman
for another lover

a woman
who dreams each night
in that other face

ELEGY FOR SONDRA

Saturday night you were one of us;
today, a sudden fear that makes us turn
our faces aside in the school corridors,
throats too tight to trust with words.

The awful silence of your dying alone,
school chants that echoed within you
only hours before at the basketball game
is a grim irony we bear — mute.

Today at the funeral the other cheerleaders
stand silent, gaudy pompoms laid aside;
the basketballers, lank, white-shirted,
shift nervously in this unfamiliar rite.

The silence of earth is now your silence,
after which there is neither dirge nor cheer;
there are other games, other silences,
but none so still as that which lingers here.

BEER AT COCHIN

The lazy August fire
                              wanted quenching.
Even the slightest breeze
                              from the lake
could not suppress the knowledge
that Cochin pub was near
and cool
      and wet.

Entering the dim-cool (alive
with beer promises) room
is so good you want to stop
                              forever
the moment
  to hang suspended.

            The Indians and Metis have their own
            section in the pub at Cochin —
            no cordons

no signs
no markers
of any kind
no nothing so blatant
but in Cochin
they know where to sit.
Everyone in the room knows
even you
total stranger
even you know too.

But you ignore it and sit down
next to a table of Indians
and wait
and it doesn't take long
no
not long at all.
Someone flips a switch
and conversation
in the room is silenced
and even the table next to you
is frozen.

And the bartender comes over
his face pained
suggesting a recent family death
and he asks
if you wouldn't like to
move closer to the bar
and you are well aware that
it really isn't a question
now
or ever.

Every time you pay attention, you praise. When that praise is uttered in a voice that is your own, it may become a poem.

— *Lorna Crozier*

Richard Stevenson was born in Victoria, B.C., and was educated at the University of Victoria and the University of British Columbia. He is a career teacher, teaching in both Canada and Nigeria. As well as being a prolific poet he is an editor of periodicals. He lives in Lethbridge and teaches at Lethbridge Community College.

WHY WERE ALL THE WEREWOLVES MEN?

Why were all the werewolves men,
with manners like my Uncle Ken:
stupid, burly mesomorphs
who preyed on women, nerds and dwarfs?

It's bad enough they ate meat raw
and left gory leftovers people saw.
With table manners so obscene,
you'd think they'd rather not be seen.

But no. They'd skulk their neighbourhoods
and leave blood trails throughout the woods,
announce their presence to the moon,
expect all women to faint and swoon,

to get all quivery and loose as liver
and fall into their arms and shiver
for the honour of offering up their flesh
to some hairy goof whose gears don't mesh.

Heck, if I were a woman and my date
broke out in fur at my front gate,
I'd take a spike heel to his head
or mace the jerk. I'd yell, "Drop dead!"

Or if night fell and a full moon
found him writhin in my room,
I'd loosen his collar at the sink,
slip him a Mickey Finn to drink.

I'd take a chisel to his pointy teeth,
haul him off to some bog or heath,
let him come to without a stitch,
fangless, hairless, in a ditch.

Let him swoon and shriek in fear
when he looks into a mirror.
Out-vamped by the feminine wiles
of a hairless were-woman who smiles

and knows how to bare her Pepsodent pearls
better than any of his goofy girls.
Someone who isn't the least impressed
by bad-breathed dweebs with hairy chests.

Gertrude Story was born on a farm near Sutherland, Saskatchewan, which is now part of Saskatoon. She is a graduate of the University of Saskatchewan. She is a poet and fiction writer and formerly a newspaper and radio journalist. She lives near Saskatoon.

MY FATHER RODE A STALLION

My father rode a stallion
and never till he died
did he know the reason why
he did.
He read the Bible,
brought his pay home
Saturdays
to the woman who ran
his kitchen,
ran messages
between pastor and priest
Sundays
to keep small town peace,
helped close down
the Fancy House
though they had a doctor
monthly
to check out all the girls.
And no one found
dirty jokes or smutty pictures
hidden in bottom drawers
when he died.

My father rode a stallion
all his life.

THE WORST PAIN

The worst pain in the world,
the men say,
sitting around the kitchen table
and putting away hot coffee
and doughnuts
fresh out of the lard,
is, Excuse them for saying it
in front of a lady,
to be kicked in the personals
by a cow pony
with her brains
all in her heels.
And the woman,
her womb torn up and
restitched
after the baby was born
dead,
dips more doughnuts,
says,
Yes, I can well imagine
that would really
hurt.

CROWS

Crows
are so black
and obvious,
they are overdone.
Overdone by God

or Darwin
or whoever painted them
in pigment
such as that;
overdone by poets
yearning to spill their guts
the not-too-obvious
way.

Crows
scavenge the eyes
even the viscera
      the gonads
      the excretions
of things dead
upon the highway.
Poets comparing themselves
to Crow
are dead
giveaways.

Don Summerhayes was born in Hamilton, Ontario. He is a graduate of McMaster University, the University of Toronto, and Yale University. He has taught at colleges and universities in both the United States and Canada including York University where he taught for many years. He lives in Toronto.

AIDE-MÉMOIRE

speak the ordinary
words clearly
without insistence

choosing to say
some common thing
we have needed to hear
over and over

if only a message
of simple greeting
we recognize
whose lives touch

and move apart

THE ONION PICKERS

My eyes water at the sight:
twenty broadhipped
kerchiefed madonnas
under the sun
of the onion fields

lolling like hussies
on the edge of the city.

They are silly as girls
and bawdy with heat
and the reek and weight
of the ribald globes
they dandle over
and over all day
in their tough hands.

Lord, how they love it —
these rowdy grandmothers
and mustachio-ed aunts
all lumps from the neck down —
away from their men!
They collapse on their sides
giddy with laughter.

One whistles at me, waving
a wicked inviting
curved knife, cupping
her hand up and up
and burlesquing
her practised lewd chop
of onion from stalk.

I think of them crowding
the innocent bus,
shedding more boldness
at each stop, but not
silent, their tongues still
purple as onions,
dresses still bulging
with smuggled beauties.

*When we have the courage to raise our eyes from the ruts of "old thought"
and look precisely at the present moment — unique, wonderful, perhaps
frightening — we are held speechless. The words, nailed down in the
patterns of old thought, are always inadequate for describing the new
moment. To capture that newness, we must invent new sound — poetry.*

— Garry Radison

Eva Tihanyi was born in Budapest, Hungary, and grew up in Windsor, Ontario. She is a graduate of the University of Windsor and has taught in many of the colleges in Toronto. Besides being a teacher and poet, she is a literary reviewer. She lives in Welland, Ontario.

URBAN SPELL

Around me the city clanks
like an officious machine
and in these confines of concrete,
among the live debris
and the delicate balances of love,
I polish the hard chrome edges
of a modern life

But today, as summer
pushed its bright yellow face
through the kitchen window,
I ran to my upstairs room
at one with the awkward symmetry
of rooftops, and felt a celebration
of towers, bridges, roads —
the elements of reaching

I grew light-headed as the sun,
something rooted in me
groping for sky, stretching

ELK LAKE IMPERATIVE

Think north

Think of blueberries in August,
the silver arrowpaths of starlight
piercing the rich red orchards
of the blood's harvest

Think of spruce, poplar, pine —
an incantation of trees
among the night-drenched rocks,
the wizardry of moonlight
on ebony green water

And remember the morning,
your bones
shifting comfortably in sunlight,
your face hot with a blush
of autumnal cold

This is the earth's secret,
the untamed song of body,
the cherished fuel
we hoard for winter

PEOPLE SAY SHE'S HYPER

People say she's hyper, well they don't know the half of it, what
goes on inside her head and for starters what does hyper mean,
there's no such word. It's doubtful that hyper would describe it
anyway, it's more like rain falling upward, her life is like that too
but that's another story, at the moment we're talking about the
contents of a head, a myriad of things and they all move at once

sometimes which of course is bound to cause collisions. Because nothing's perfect, not even thoughts in the head — least of all thoughts in the head — so she ends up thinking about things even when she doesn't want to, thought happens despite all effort, and sometimes it's interesting and sometimes it's not and sometimes it makes her hyper but being hyper (people say) won't help distinguish which is which. In fact people say she shouldn't think because she's dangerous then, which is what it all comes down to in the end, doesn't it, danger and the fear of it.

MY MOTHER TURNS 50

As another year of silence
falls from the calendar,
I imagine her exploring malls,
reading cheap romances, staring
for hours at air, photo albums,
the drafting degree
beside the welfare cheque;
imagine her taut gaiety
braced for breaking,
her body fat with boredom
massed in front of me,
obstacle, reminder

Ten years since he left
yet love for my father
still ticks in her heart
like a perfect clock,
timeless

I imagine peeling
the decade from her face,
finding her as she was
and somehow understanding

THE CHILD EVENTUALLY GROWS UP

At six months
you tossed me into my grandmother's arms
like a basketball to the nearest teammate,
then ran from the court

The two of you — my mother, my father —
in your hopeful daring twenties
haycarting across the Hungarian border
in the January night

Too much risk with an infant
you thought, and we all survived

Six years later
you collected me at the airport,
a long-lost suitcase, contents
not remembered

What you found was, in your view,
mouthy, clumsy, undignified;
a child in need of lessons

And so you forced me to the top bunk
to cure my fear of heights,
cut my hair short enough
to ensure it could no longer hold
my grandmother's ribbons
(you said I needed style)

I was not like my four-year-old brother,
by birth an instant North American kid
to match the Campbell's soup,
the chrome and plastic furniture

What I was you did not want —
a small self
flying open-souled and curious
to her faraway fairytale parents
who now expect
all they could not give

PRENATAL CLASS

They say:

> It's important to discuss procedures —
> shave, enema, intravenous, epidural,
> breastfeeding, possible Caesarean

> Don't let yourself be bullied

> Know what you want

> Be firm

They say:

> Eat well, get exercise, prepare

> Learn how to rest, breathe, control
> the body's involuntary whims

> Be ready

What they don't say:

> When finally you hold him, head
> still blood-crusted, hands
> smallest starfish on your belly,
> the pain over, just beginning,
> there is a love beyond love

Know this

I like to think of poems as small mysteries, living knots of experience and emotion that cannot exist in any other form. A poem is its own answer, its own joy, its own tragedy.

— *Andrew Wreggitt*

Tom Wayman was born in Hawkesbury, Ontario. He is a graduate
of the University of British Columbia and the University of Cali-
fornia. He has held various teaching positions in colleges and
universities in both the United States and Canada. He has been
publishing books of poetry and anthologies for a quarter of a
century. Wayman is the Squire of Appledore, an estate in the
Selkirk Mountains of southeastern British Columbia.

METRIC CONVERSION

Looking through his poems one day
Wayman suddenly stops, astonished. Just before a line
about driving 450 miles
a highway sign has been erected: two wooden posts painted green
and a thin metal rectangle which states *724 kilometres.*

Wayman flips ahead. Further on
in front of a mention of 300 pounds
another construction announces *136.36 kilograms.*
This sign is even fresher: the green paint
is still tacky when Wayman pokes it with his finger.

Wayman turns directly to a certain poem he remembers
and, sure enough, before a clause that reads
"the temperature was forty degrees"
two wooden posts, unpainted, are stuck into the ground.
On a piece of metal leaning against them, Wayman sees
4 degrees Celsius. And nearby on the grass
two men are eating lunch
surrounded by their tools, cans of paint, lumber and sawhorses.

"What are you doing here?" Wayman asks. "Eating lunch,"
one of the men replies calmly.

"Listen," Wayman says, "I don't want your signs in my poems."
"Are these your poems?" the man asks, looking up.
"Yes," Wayman says. The two men stare at him, chewing thoughtfully.

TRAVELLING COMPANIONS

At the bus station in Winnipeg,
buying a ticket for Winkler, Manitoba,
Wayman hears a familiar voice behind him:
"Make that two to Winkler." Wayman turns, and
it's Four Letter Word.
"I told you to stay back at the hotel,"
Wayman says. "I'll only be gone for a day.
It's a high school reading
and they asked me specifically not to bring you."
"Nonsense," Four Letter Word says,
reaching past Wayman to pay his portion of the fares.

"You're not welcome there," Wayman insists,
as he struggles out to the bus
with his suitcase and a big box of books to sell.
"That's not the point," Wayman's companion replies
as they hand their tickets to the driver
and climb up into the vehicle.
"Next you'll be ordered not to read
poems that mention smoking or drinking."

"I don't think you understand," Wayman begins
while the bus threads its way through the five o'clock traffic
and out onto the endless frozen prairie.
"The organizers of this program
asked me not to cause any trouble.
It seems somebody like you was brought into a school last year
and there were complaints all the way to the Minister of Education."

Four Letter Word stares out a window
at the darkening expanse of white snow.
"And you're the guy," he says at last,
"who's always telling people
I'm the one that gives the language its richness and vitality.
Didn't Wordsworth declare
poets should speak in the language of real men and women?"

"But it's a high school," Wayman tries to interject.
"Do you think the kids don't swear?" his friend asks.
"Or their parents? And I didn't want to bring this up,"
he continues, "but you depend on me. You use me for good reasons
and without me your performance will flop."
"No, it won't," Wayman says.
"It will," his companion asserts.
And the two ride through the deep winter night
in an unpleasant silence.

An hour later, they pull into the lights of Winkler
and here's the school librarian
waiting in the cold at the bus stop.
"You must be Wayman," he says
as Wayman steps down. "And is this a friend of yours?"
"I never saw him before in my life," Wayman responds
but his companion is already shaking hands with the librarian.
"So good to be here," he says, picking up Wayman's box of books.
"Now, when do we read?"

WAYMAN IN LOVE

At last Wayman gets the girl into bed.
He is locked in one of those embraces
so passionate his left arm is asleep
when suddenly he is bumped in the back.
"Excuse me," a voice mutters, thick with German.

Wayman and the girl sit up astounded
as a furry gentleman in boots and a frock coat
climbs in under the covers.

"My name is Doktor Marx," the intruder announces
settling his neck comfortably on the pillow.
"I'm here to consider for you the cost of a kiss."
He pulls out a notepad. "Let's see now,
we have the price of the mattress, this room must be rented,
your time off work, groceries for two,
medical fees in case of accidents . . . . "

"Look," Wayman says,
"couldn't we do this later?"
The philosopher sighs, and continues: "You are affected too, Miss.
If you are not working, you are going to resent
your dependent position. This will influence
I assure you, your most intimate moments . . . . "

"Doctor, please," Wayman says. "All we want
is to be left alone."
But another beard, more nattily dressed,
is also getting into the bed.
There is a shifting and heaving of bodies
as everyone wriggles out room for themselves.
"I want you to meet a friend from Vienna,"
Marx says. "This is Doktor Freud."

The newcomer straightens his glasses,
peers at Wayman and the girl.
"I can see," he begins,
"that you two have problems . . . . "

DEAD END

Feeling morbid in the Spring, Wayman figures
it's time to get ready. He pours himself another coffee
pads over to his desk and begins.
If I should die, think only this of me:
There is some corner of a field somewhere
That is forever Wayman . . . It strikes him suddenly
this has been done. He tries again.
The laws of probability tell us
that every breath we take contains some molecules
from the last gasp of Julius Caesar. Think about that.
At this very moment you may be breathing
some of Wayman's too . . . .

This seems awfully long-winded. Wayman recalls a friend
who refused to read anything longer than a page.
And a newspaper editor who howled at him:
"If you can't say it in a paragraph, forget it."
Remember me this way, Wayman decides:

Say of Wayman's end, as he said himself
of so many unfortunate things that happened to him while he lived:
At least
he got a poem out of it.

Poetry is such a refined communication that it sometimes walks the fine
line between understanding and disdain.

— *Peter Christensen*

Lyle Weis was born in Beardmore, Ontario. He is a graduate of Simon Fraser University, the University of British Columbia and the University of Alberta. A former teacher, lecturer and arts administrator, he now divides his time between writing poetry, fiction or articles and teaching writing workshops. He lives in Edmonton.

THE MILL UNDER HIS SKIN

So there came to be at least one farmer
who carried his rage to work in a lunch bucket
his initials scratched deep and crude
past black paint to glinting steel

During graveyard evenings at the plywood mill
the passing sheets of wood became landscapes
hills and gullies brown as summer

His body found no rhythm here
his parts were forced across the grain:
    nostrils rubbed raw by
    smell of glue and sap
        fingers worn hard by
        endless lumber and board
            spirit rubbed to pulp by
            memories of his land
lost
    along with the gentle cattle
    the cleanly plowed soil
        the sweet alfalfa air

He came home one morning with the sun
and a long sliver nestled tight
and purple under his forearm skin,

shouted *Get away!*
to a wife's nervous hands
sat down with a knife and candle
and smiled

At last
his work was his own again:
the hand, remembering, would
      cut   slice   pick
the mill from his body

AN OPEN LETTER TO A SERIOUS WRITER

Sure,
writing for kids is easy
all you have to do
is a backflip in time
make your voice change
forget pre-tense
remember present tense

Reel in the nets of wonder
the sky embedded with our shouts
the woods alive with our shadows
the earth still trembling under our feet

No problem
as you step into that fertile zone
simply grab a handful of spring airs
inhale those words so lately spoken

Try it sometime
But first
fill your pockets with bread crumbs
before you enter those woods

BLACK WIDOW

I lifted the stone to find her
poised in black silk
the hourglass blazing on her waist

I had stumbled into her bedroom
and now wondered
Will you sting me?

She hesitated, considering,
her sleek black body ready
as she leaned against a pebble
with long slender legs crossed:
the older woman measuring the boy

Dusky, confident, she waited on
this new suitor, he so
tantalizingly near
deliciously large
while her certainty allowed
my hand to move slowly away

No doubt she understood
better than any other
the rock that crushed her

ICARUS IN THE OKANAGAN

No feathers to flutter helpless to water
    but red and white stitched nylon sails
No wax warm and dripping in the sun
    but strong light aluminum tubing
No young muscles excited to the blue
      but a Chrysler inboard with dual ports
      backwashing noise against trembling
      apple leaves across the lakeland valley

This is all we ask for a hero now
      a lycra-loined sailor gripping a tow rope
      and stepping from water skis as speed mounts
      a youth riding the wings of modern invention
      rising to the darkening sky

Unnoticed by the cheering shore crowd
      the evening sun that once had means to melt
    weakly lights the sailor's safe descent
    into a nest of waves
          the shrunken disk of glory
             slumps bruised and cooling
                behind the echoing hills

HAWK IN THE SNOW

I came down from the hills
a dark figure growing larger
whipping snow wands with my skis

Came to rest on the trail
where he stood
head smeared with blood:

a hawk perched on the shredded chest
of a pheasant only moments dead

Hard beak
        clicking on bone
                                tearing tendons
                ripping guts
steam rose above
red-flecked snow

His deep globe of eye
        flicked up
        fixed me
neck-snapping collision in midair

No use to twist away
        everything around me
snow sky hills shadows and light —
                every   thing
was pulled rushing and roaring
air whistling
into the vortex
of his eye

I stood hovering
        fixed
he moved slightly
gripping tightly
the mess under his claws:
it was his and I . . .

I turned on thin slivers of wood
        slipped down the trail
                a slim figure retreating
shrinking away
from that eye

VIGIL

Come on
get up
you don't wear these well
the tubes tie you down
the backless gown ruins a boy's dignity

In this sterile room
you seem always ready
to leave us
as if none of our urgings
would be strong enough to hold
should you say goodbye

This is not your place
where the hall echoes at 2 am
to the steady machine at your side

Yours is the sun pulling morning to the trees
the whir of tires on the pavement
the dew of grass on your knees

Come back son
play with me under the open skies
and I will be the boy with you
a promise built on these hours
become minutes
we could have shared

George Whipple was born in Saint John, New Brunswick, and grew
up in Toronto. He is a graduate of the Vancouver Teachers College.
He lives in Burnaby, B.C.

INNOCENCE

When autumn scents
invoke a kind of déjà-vu
(of being in some garden
from before the Fall)
behind each Senior High
— completely unaware
they breathe that stolen air
reserved for innocence,
stands always a young me
holding a youthful *you*.

When evening comes
they wander to a place
where a ripe apple bends
above them like a moon:
and having tested it,
they tidy up a bit,
returning to their friends
with solemn steps and slow,
warm fingers intertwined
and in a sort of daze.

INDIAN SUMMER

I wade through blood.
A regiment of bones
crackles underfoot:
October's mortars pound
the scarlet-coated wood.

(Each death's a birth.
Tear down a theatre,
reveal a church.
Tear down the church,
reveal the perfect sky.)

There is no choice.
The colour guard
of autumn charges on
till winter says depart,
and spring exclaims, Rejoice!

ASTROPHYSICS

To liberate a stone
we plant the moon with flags
— and all the while, philandering,
the bee extends deep down, deep down
into the tickled, pink, arched funnel of the rose
his large impenitent furred thighs
hung with bulging saddle-bags.

The sticky, sly components of a future rose
he bears into the lucid blue perfume
of Aprils yet to come.
Though winter's almost here
spring never ends.

THE WRITING ON THE WALL

In my zombie teens
I froze my blood with thumbed
and dog-eared phantoms, Frankensteins
conjured out of pocket money, dread, and pulp
that stunk of printer's ink and howling tombs
where Golems, geeks and dybbuks brought to life
my drooling eyes — ah, sweet mystery of death.

But now I see Time's writing on the wall.
We are born to die. The fallen tree
regenerates from loam a new perfection
as winds revise the clouds — forever
woven and unwoven in the air.

Up the long south-western slope of understanding,
lamenting that the conference of ghouls
had gathered only briefly
to remind my freedom of its end
(I no longer trust in what *The Shadow* knows)
I go to my correction, embarrassed by regret,
presentiments — the old man's tic of tears.

PASSING THROUGH EDEN

Something flashes
at the corner of your eye
sometimes as circumspect as gossamer
yet it will haunt you all your life:
a window white
with cherry blossoms —
1938.
And north of nowhere, once,
a winding road at dusk,
the glitter of a cold, black pond:
four cows browsing in the grass.

Such simple things remember us —
half-open doors through which we glimpse
the aboriginal first place
where Adam, wide-eyed, rose
and saw the first morning breaking
on the red, primordial, first rose.

THE PRODIGAL

Fresh playground voices —
like the rose they too
shall wither in the
winter weather and no
Persephone of wounded stone
will cure the sun
dying in the eyes of squirrels
who wait their sister, snow.

Where autumn hangs the year
from blood-stained trees
I take my soul
for its evening walk.

And when the shadows lengthen
I hope to see the one
who is both star, astronomer —
as through a bedroom window once
I saw our neighbour in the middle of
the night turn all the houselights on
for someone coming home from far away.

Andrew Wreggitt was born in Sudbury, Ontario. He is a graduate of the University of British Columbia. Besides writing poetry, Wreggitt has a distinguished career writing for CBC radio and television drama over the past three decades. He lives in Calgary.

SONNY LISTON

The Photograph:

If there was a photograph of that moment,
you would see
a boy about seven years old
He is wearing jeans and a short-sleeved shirt,
the yellow diamonds on his brown socks
descend like stars
into black and white sneakers
The boy is lying on an orange couch,
in front of him is a blank television screen
and slightly to the left,
a radio with lighted numbers on the band
The boy is listening intently to something,
hands cupped behind his head,
elbows pointed out
To one side, you might notice
a shadow falling over the arm-rest of the couch
The shadow is faint and barely
visible to the camera
but it is also part of the picture

What You Cannot See:

The boy is listening to a boxing match
between Cassius Clay and Sonny Liston

He doesn't know who the fighters are,
that they are in another country
or even that they are fighting each other for money
 He has stumbled upon them by accident,
attracted by the frenetic announcers
and the rumble of the crowd
The boy is not listening to a fight
between two people,
he is imagining two names,
Cassius Clay and Sonny Liston
He feels the two c's of Cassius Clay
raking the bright, round sun
of Sonny Liston
He has imagined himself as the sound
of Sonny Liston, the sibilance of the s's
and the long oh's
He is suddenly tense and anxious
the way he often is at school,
the vowels of his silences, inarticulate
the sibilant shouts of children
The same moment, Sonny Liston staggers against the ropes
in the sixth round at Miami Beach
The boy feels himself pressed onto the orange couch
by a sound, the idea of Sonny Liston,
the sound of his name being knocked down
through the boy, this row of lights and numbers
The boxer raises both hands to his head
and leans forward with a body shot
What you cannot see:
The shadow that falls on the arm of the couch
belongs to the boy's mother
She has approached from the next room,
the hall light casting only a dim shadow
in the early evening
She is tired and has been waiting
for her husband to come home,

looking out the window
for the turn of his headlights
She is about to speak
as her shadow touches the frame of the picture
but there is a shout from the radio
and she stops to listen, her eyes fixed
on the face of the small boy, rigid, drained
Sonny Liston reels to the canvas

After:

The woman moves easily
across the space where the photograph
might have been,
her shadow sliding quickly across the room
to the boy's face
She gathers him up from the orange couch
her body blocking the hysterical radio,
cutting off the small lights and numbers
She is glad to feel the boy's arms
around her neck
The moments are pushed ahead,
lifted from the orange couch
The porch light is flicked on,
a flash of headlights in the driveway
Sonny Liston spits out his mouthpiece
and refuses to answer the bell for the seventh round
The boy lies in his soft blankets
nearly asleep, saying Sonny Liston's name
over and over in his head,
the small lights of the radio
burning like phosphorous
in his memory

CARS

Driving with my father in Vancouver
the summer before he died,
the city's hum and exhaust
laying its warm hands on us,
the breath of the city
with its radios and going-home promise
The traffic grinds
like a slow metallic animal
undulating on its narrow track,
all of us trusting it
to take us anywhere, unknowing,
the animal we belong to

In our family, there was a different car every week
Sometimes cars only lasted
a day before my father sold them
Chryslers with flying tail fins,
or Mustangs with tail lights
like puzzled clown faces
brightening at the end of the driveway
Mostly, they were plain Ford Fairlanes,
Comets and Galaxies,
trade-ins that still held traces
of other families, other children
gawking out back windows
I investigated each one
when it came home,
opening and closing doors,
wondering always if this was the car
that would stay,
the car that would sit in the driveway
every weekend,

the one I would recognize
on the street, driving past,
my father in his suit
and hat just so

I envied the cars of my friends
whose parents came and went in them
with regular hours,
my friends who could say
"this is our car"
and all that went with that,
the ownership,
the security of a large object
always there in the driveway
As if it was a dog,
as if it could love you back

My father smiles as we ride
in the mechanical river, gears and tires,
each with its singular cargo
My home, the city I believed
was somehow different, wiser
than the one I grew up in
Still not understanding,
all those years, my father refusing to be defined
by the technology that drove us,
the pile of metal in the driveway,
recognizing the current that sweeps us
as human, not metal and rubber
Only now, I realize this is my last
image of him, leaning back in the passenger seat,
window open, the blare of summer heat
The imperfect machine of memory
we bring home to our own families,
the traces of love we search for,
opening and closing its gentle doors

BURNING MY FATHER'S CLOTHES

Burning my father's clothes
in a metal drum behind the house,
my mother afraid to give them away,
afraid to see them walking by on a stranger
The oily black smoke coils
up through the trees
and out across the snow-covered hills

Here is the coat I remember
from the trip we took
to somewhere
I am lying in the back seat,
my mother asleep in the passenger side
Headlights flashing in his face,
he drives all night like this
in the silence of our sleeping
The world was safe and dark and intimate
His solitude with the white lines,
the flat prairie, the eyes of deer
sparkling in the ditches
and the dull glow of some city
still an hour's drive away
Waking up to see him there and I remember
even the smell of this coat, tobacco,
these deep closets of memory

Burning my father's clothes
The only child
standing in the snow and smoke and silence
I pile the shirts and jackets on
and the orange flames strike at them
over and over

The smoke billows up
and everything is given to the sky,
unwilling and stubborn,
ashes settling on the shoulders
of my own coat

The smoke sweeps through the trees
and up into the hills we worked together,
across the fence we built
And there is not a bird in this thicket,
no rabbits, or mice pushing through the new snow
Nothing moves or grows or mourns
for anything lost here
Only the smoke of my father's clothes,
spiralling up,
then falling in the cold air . . .

the face of my mother
anxious
hovering in the window

BENEDICTION

An old man bargains for coffee
in the early morning diner
His cupped hands hold coins
not enough for breakfast
or even a refill
"It's Good Friday" he tells the waitress
"Christ was crucified today"
She nods

The old man recounts yesterday's accident
"A boy on a bicycle, hit by a red Mazda,
just a young kid"
The waitress turns, her frown in the pie case

"I didn't see it, but it happened just on the corner there"
His hands surround the empty cup

I watch from the counter,
my face an odd reflection
among the day-old pies
I have wandered here in the still morning
dragged away by the snarled
traffic of my sleep
The old man waits
for the benediction of the waitress

His face turned up
Good Friday
"I have only thirteen cents"
The empty morning
filled with this knowledge
"They say it was a red Mazda"
Echo of blood, the smooth
stones of his eyes
She fills his cup, "This is the last one okay?"
He says nothing, his faced turned up to her
My own face in the pie rack

Good Friday,
I am thinking of a red Mazda, a bicycle
the young boy

ELEANOR, FRASER LAKE

It is Eleanor
who breaks down weeping
in an aisle at Supervalu, the cart
full of groceries
her children asking, "what's wrong?"
but she cannot answer

There is no one answer
to give

. . . because I am bone weary all the time
and cannot sleep,
because my husband is not working
and won't look anymore
because the television won't stop
criticizing me, and I can't shut it off
because I'm sick of hearing about closures
and who is moving away next
because of all the places and times
to come apart,
like a thread pulled from a sweater,
suddenly there is nothing more sad or tragic to me
than this row of detergent boxes,
these worn bare tiles,
the awful sight of myself
trapped in the round mirror
on the ceiling

AT THE WEDDING

The old farmer sits on the stage of the community hall
His feet dangle like plumb lines,
thick black shoes
swaying slowly to the music
His boys are on the dance floor
Their blond heads stick out in the crowd
like shafts of wheat
Five of them, the last one married today,
all of them living in different cities

He remembers each of them, fighting him,
running off to become what they are,

salesmen, doctors, city-dwellers
Even now, the old suspicion still in their faces
Quick to argue
over chores or raising children
He watches them moving in their white shirts,
their wives smiling and small children
tugging at their pant-legs

He knows now that he loved them
impossibly, for the arguments and the hard words
for being young and insolent
like a field of stones coaxed into grain
He wonders if they love him the same way,
with hindsight, with a farmer's suspicion of elements,
the unsureness they learned from him

He wishes now that one of them
would come and sit with him
up here on the stage,
touch his shoulder and talk
about the farm, or anything
He wishes now that he had loved them
always, as surely
as he loves them now

YOUNGEST IN CANADA

Brent, fifteen years old
stands in the door of his parents' house
"I'm goin loggin in a month
Drove a cat last summer, youngest in Canada"
Each word is a challenge thrown at my feet
All down the block
his stereo shakes ravens out of trees
The song says "I don't like you, I don't

like you . . . "
his arms crossed in a knot
against his chest

He startles me with his sureness, his stern face,
the tough frame he has built for his life
His faith is a sleek car
paid for in one summer,
this rumble of drums and guitars,
a coat he wears against the world

Behind him in the harbour
freighters gather up his labour
quotas of wood
What they give back,
new tires, stereos,
"I don't like you, I don't like you . . . "
An inventory of years on the vibrating machines,
what they give back to anyone

I go home and the music drives on
the way Brent's days will crash
one after another down the slopes of these mountains,
his anger growing for years until it is too big
for music, fast cars,
until the faith is broken

Tonight, he is the youngest in Canada,
his challenge batters the neighbourhood
We who have lived longer in the world
close our windows, the simple beliefs gone out of us,
our anger an older, harder song

FISHING

A mother and son
stand by a river in autumn,
yellow hills
heavy with the rich smell of leaves
In the early morning
they share a fishing rod
and a thermos of coffee

All around them the air is full
of the father's absence
The huge space that he left
swallows up the hills,
the sky, the hungry river
Everything pulls away from the touch

The woman takes her turn with the rod,
tosses the small gold lure
out on the water
It sweeps across the current, flashing
a long graceful arc
She stands with her son
pulling the lure in again
with slow turns of her hand

The son sits on a rock
drinking coffee, his hat pulled low
like his father's
He knows a fish will rise to the gold lure
that the hills will shake off
the cold dew of morning
His mother turns
and smiles at him over her shoulder
afraid and sorrowful

needing to see him
the familiar angle of his hat
He smiles back
the river behind her alive with sunlight

Slowly, they begin
to fill the vast morning

*Poetry always means the possibility of change. Even the finished text is
not final.*

— Don Summerhayes

BERT ALMON

The Return and Other Poems (San Marcos Press, 1968); *Taking Possession* (Solo Press, 1976); *Poems for the Nuclear Family* (San Marcos Press, 1979); *Blue Sunrise* (Thistledown Press, 1980); *Deep North* (Thistledown Press, 1984); *Calling Texas* (Thistledown Press, 1990); *Earth Prime* (Brick Books, 1994); *Mind the Gap* (Ekstasis Editions, 1996).

ALLAN BARR

The Chambered Nautilus (Thistledown Press, 1992)

DOUG BEARDSLEY

Going Down Into History (Oolichan Press, 1976); *The Only Country in the World Called Canada* (Sesame Press, 1976); *Six Saanich Poems* (Victoria Indian Cultural Education Centre, 1977); *Play on the Water: The Paul Klee Poems* (Press Porcepic, 1978); *Poems* (with Charles Lillard) (Islomane Press, 1979); *Pacific Sands* (League of Canadian Poets Pamphlet, 1980); *Kissing the Body of My Lord: The Marie Poems* (Longspoon Press, 1982); *A Dancing Star* (Thistledown Press, 1988); *Free to Talk* (Hawthorne Press, 1992); *Inside Passage* (Thistledown Press, 1993); *Wrestling With Angels* (Signal Hill Edtions, 1995).

BRIAN BRETT

Fossil Ground at Phantom Creek (Blackfish, 1976); *Smoke Without Exit* (Sono Nis Press, 1984); *Evolution In Every Direction* (Thistledown Press, 1987); *Poems: New and Selected* (Sono Nis Press, 1943); *Allegories of Love and Disaster* (Exile Editions, 1993); *The Colour of Bones In A Stream* (Sono Nis Press, 1998).

CATHERINE M. BUCKAWAY

Strangely the Birds Have Come (Fiddlehead Poetry Books, 1973); *Air 17* (A Bryte Raven Production, 1973); *The Silver Cuckoo* (Borealis Press, 1975); *The Lavender Nightingale* (Peppermint, 1978); *Waiting for George* (Abraxis Press, 1985); *Blue Windows: New & Selected Poems* (Coteau Books, l985);

Stardust (The Plowman, 1989); *Riding Into Morning* (Thistledown Press, 1989),

GREG BUTTON

Inside of Midnight (Thistledown Press, 1993).

ANNE CAMPBELL

No Memory of a Move (Longspoon Press, 1983); *Death Is An Anxious Mother* (Thistledown Press, 1986); *Red Earth, Yellow Stone* (Thistledown Press, 1989); *Angel Wings All Over* (Thistledown Press, 1994).

KEN CATHERS

Images On Water (Oolichan Books, 1976); *Outward Voyage* (Oolichan Books, 1980); *Sanctuary* (Thistledown Press, 1991); *World of Strangers* (Ekstasis Editions, 1997).

MARILYN CAY

Farm (Thistledown Press, 1993).

LESLEY CHOYCE

Re-Inventing the Wheel (Fiddlehead Poetry Books, 1980); *Fast Living* (Fiddlehead Poetry Books, 1982); *The End of Ice* (Fiddlehead Poetry Books, 1985); *The Top of the Heart* (Thistledown Press, 1986); *The Man Who Borrowed the Bay of Fundy* (Brandon University [Dollar Poems]; 1988); *The Coastline of Forgetting* (Pottersfield Press, 1995); *Nova Scotia: Shaped by the Sea* (Penguin Books, 1996); *Dance the Rocks Ashore* (Goose Lane Editions, 1997).

PETER CHRISTENSEN

Hail Storm (Thistledown Press, 1977); *Rig Talk* (Thistledown Press, 1981); *To Die Ascending* (Thistledown Press, 1988).

JOHN LIVINGSTONE CLARK

Stepping Up to the Station (Coteau Books,1990); *Breakfart of the Magi* (Thistledown Press, 1994); *Prayers and Other Unfinished Letters* (Exile Editions, 1995); *Passage to Indigo* (Exile Editions, 1996); *Back to Bethany:*

eighty nine paragraphs about jesus and lazarus in abbotsford (Exile Editions, 1997).

CHRIS COLLINS

Earthworks (Thistledown Press, 1990).

DENNIS COOLEY

Leaving (Turnstone Press, 1980); *Fielding* (Thistledown Press, 1983); *Bloody Jack* (Turnstone Press, 1984); *Soul Searching* (Red Deer College Press, 1987); *Dedications* (Thistledown Press, 1988); *Perishable Light* (Coteau Books, 1988); *This Only Home: Poems* (Turnstone Press, 1992); *Burglar of Blood* (Pachyderm, 1992); *gold finger* (Staccato, 1995); *Sunfall: New and Selected Poems, 1980-1996* (House of Anansi, 1996).

LORNA CROZIER

Inside is the Sky (Thistledown Press, 1976); *Crow's Black Joy* (NeWest Press, 1979); *Humans and Other Beasts* (Turnstone Press, 1980); *No Longer Two People* (with Patrick Lane) (Turnstone Press, 1981); *The Weather* (Coteau Books, 1983); *The Garden Going On Without Us* (McClelland & Stewart, 1985); *Angels of Flesh, Angels of Silence* (McClelland & Stewart, 1988); *Inventing the Hawk* (McClelland & Stewart, 1992); *Everything Arrives at the Light* (McClelland & Stewart, 1995); *A Saving Grace: The Collected Poems of Mrs. Bentley* (McClelland & Stewart, 1996).

MICHAEL CULLEN

Heritage of the Speckled Bird (Poorhouse Press, 1975); *The Curried Chicken Apocalypse* (Thistledown Press, 1979).

LORNE DANIEL

The Hunting Hand (Red Deer College Press, 1973); *Towards a New Compass* (Thistledown Press, 1978); *Falling Together* (Thistledown Press, 1986); *In the Flesh* (Sidereal Press, 1988).

H.C. DILLOW

Orts and Scantlings (Thistledown Press, 1984).

PAULETTE DUBÉ

the house weighs heavy (Thistledown Press, 1992); *playing the hand* (Black Moss Press, 1996).

PATRICK FRIESEN

the lands i am (Turnstone Press, 1976); *bluebottle* (Turnstone Press, 1978); *The Shunning* (Turnstone Press, 1980); *Unearthly Horses* (Turnstone Press, 1984); *Flicker and Hawk* (Turnstone Press, 1987); *You Don't Get to be a Saint* (Turnstone Press, 1992); *Blasphemer's Wheel* (Turnstone Press, 1994); *A Broken Bowl* (Turnstone Press, 1997); *St. Mary at Main* (The Muses' Company, 1998).

LEONA GOM

Kindling (Fiddlehead Poetry Books, 1972); *The Singletree* (Sono Nis Press, 1975); *Land of the Peace* (Thistledown Press, 1980); *Northbound* (Thistledown Press, 1984); *Private Properties* (Sono Nis Press, 1986); *The Collected Poems, 1991* (Sono Nis Press, 1991).

JIM GREEN

North Book (Blackfish Press, 1975; Polestar Press, 1986); *Beyond Here* (Thistledown Press, 1983).

HELEN HAWLEY

Gathering Fire (Thistledown Press, 1977); *Credo* (Earthright, UK, 1983); *Grasshopper* (Turnstone Press, 1984).

JOHN V. HICKS

Now is a Far Country (Thistledown Press, 1978); *Winter Your Sleep* (Thistledown Press, 1980); *Silence Like the Sun* (Thistledown Press, 1983); *Rootless Tree* (Thistledown Press, 1985); *Fives and Sixes* (The Porcupine's Quill, 1986); *Sticks and Strings: Selected and New Poems* (Thistledown Press, 1988); *Month's Mind* (Thistledown Press, 1992); *Overheard by Conifers* (Thistledown Press, 1996); *Renovated Rhymes* (Groundwood Books, 1997).

GERALD HILL

Heartwood (Thistledown Press, 1985).

ROBERT HILLES

Look the Lovely Animal Speaks (Turnstone Press, 1980); *The Surprise Element* (Sidereal Press, 1982); *An Angel in the Works* (Oolichan Books, 1983); *Outlasting the Landscape* (Thistledown Press, 1989); *Finding the Lights On* (Wolsak and Wynn, 1991); *A Breath at a Time* (Oolichan Books, 1992); *Cantos from a Small Room* (Wolsak and Wynn, 1993); *Nothing Vanishes* (Wolsak and Wynn, 1996); *Breathing Distance* (Black Moss Press, 1997).

DORIS HILLIS

The Prismatic Eye (Thistledown Press, 1985); *Wheelings* (Thistledown Press, 1995).

LEWIS HORNE

The Seventh Day (Thistledown Press, 1982).

BRUCE HUNTER

Selected Canadian Rifles (Unfinished Monument Press, 1981); *Benchmark* (Thistledown Press, 1982); *The Beekeeper's Daughter* (Thistledown Press, 1986).

GARY HYLAND

Poems From a Loft (Anak Press, 1974); *Home Street* (Coteau Books, 1975); *Just Off Main* (Thistledown Press, 1982); *Street of Dreams* (Coteau Books, 1984); *After Atlantis* (Thistledown Press, 1991); *White Crane Spreads Wings* (Coteau Books, 1996).

SHERRY JOHNSON

Pale Grace (Thistledown Press, 1996).

PATRICK LANE

Letters From the Savage Mind (Very Stone House, 1966); *Separations* (New/Books, 1969); *On the Street* (Very Stone House, 1970); *Hiway 401 Rhapsody* (Very Stone House, 1971); *The Sun Has Begun to Eat the Mountain* (Ingluvin, 1972); *Passing Into Storm* (Traumerei Communications, 1973); *Beware the Months of Fire* (House of Anansi Press, 1974); *Unborn Things: South American Poems* (Madeira Park, 1975); *Albino Pheasants* (Harbour

Publishing, 1977); *Poems: New & Selected* (Oxford University Press, 1978); *No Longer Two People* (with Lorna Crozier) (Tumstone Press, 1979); *The Measure* (Black Moss Press, 1980); *Old Mother* (Oxford University Press, 1982); *Woman in the Dust* (Mosaic Press, 1983); *A Linen Crow, A Caftan Magpie* (Thistledown Press, 1985); *Selected Poems* (Oxford University Press, 1987); *Winter* (Coteau Books, 1990); *Mortal Remains* (Exile Editions, 1991); *Too Spare, Too Fierce* (Harbour Publishing, 1995); *Selected Poems 1977-1997* (Harbour Publishing, 1997).

WILLIAM LATTA

Summer's Bright Blood (Thisdedown Press, 1976); *Drifting Into Grey* (Four Humours Press, 1977); *Number Facts* (League of Canadian Poets Sampler, 1980).

SHELLEY A. LEEDAHL

A Few Words for January (Thistledown Press, 1990).

JOHN LENT

A Rock Solid (Dreadnaught, 1978); *Wood Lake Music* (Harbour Publishing, 1982); *Frieze* (Thistledown Press, 1984); *The Face In the Garden* (Thistledown Press, 1990).

MARK LOWEY

Forgetting How to Fly (Thistledown Press, 1987).

KIM MALTMAN

The Country of Mapmakers (Fiddlehead Poetry Books, 1977); *Branch Lines* (Thistledown Press, 1982); *The Transparence of November Snow* (with Roo Borson) (Quarry Press, 1985); *The Sickness of Hats* (Fiddlehead Poetry Books, 1985); *Technologies/Installations* (Brick Books, 1990),

DAVE MARGOSHES

Walking at Brighton (Thistledown Press, 1988); *Northwest Passage* (Oberon Press, 1990); *Fables of Creation* (Black Moss Press, 1997).

RHONA MCADAM

Life in Glass (Longspoon Press, 1984); *Hour of the Pearl* (Thistledown Press, 1987); *Creating the Country* (Thistledown Press, 1989); *Old Habits* (Thistledown Press, 1993 [Co-published with Slowdancer Press, UK]).

COLIN MORTON

In Transit (Thistledown Press, 1981); *Printed Matter* (Sidereal Press, 1982); *This Won't Last Forever* (Longspoon Press, 1985); *The Merzbook: Kurt Schwitter's Poems* (Quarry Press, 1987); *How to Be Born Again* (Quarry Press, 1992); *Oceans Apart* (Quarry Press, 1995); *Mood Indigo: Poems in the Key of Blue* (Grove Avenue Press, 1996); *Coastlines of the Archipelago* (Quarry Press, 1998).

BRENDA NISKALA

Ambergris Moon (Thistledown Press, 1983); *Open 24 Hours* (with four other poets) (Broken Jaw Press, 1997).

CHARLES NOBLE

Unfounded Knowledge (Anak, 1972); *Three* (with Jon Whyte and J.O. Thompson) (Summerthought, 1973); *Haywire Rainbow* (Press Porcepic, 1978); *Afternoon Starlight* (Thistledown Press, 1984); *Banff/breaking* (Longspoon Press, 1984); *Let's Hear it for Them* (Thistledown Press, 1990); *Wormwood Vermouth, Warphistory* (Thistledown Press, 1995).

PETER ORMSHAW

The Purity of Arms (Thistledown Press, 1993).

DON POLSON

Wakening (Fiddlehead Poetry Press, 1971); *Brief Evening in a Catholic Hospital* (Fiddlehead Poetry Press, 1972); *In Praise of Young Thieves* (Alive Press, 1975); *Lone Travellers* (Fiddlehead Poetry Press, 1979); *Moving Through Deep Snow* (Thistledown Press, 1984); *And Though It Is Not Death* (Wee Giant Press, 1986).

GARRY RADISON

Eye of a Stranger (Coteau Books, 1978); *White Noise* (Thistledown Press, 1982); *Songs of the Elephant Man* (Thingvalla Press, 1986); *Jeffers' Skull* (Cormorant Books, 1988).

MONTY REID

Fridays (Sidereal Press, 1979); *Karst Means Stone* (NeWest Press, 1979); *The Life of Ryley* (Thistledown Press, 1981); *The Dream of Snowy Owls* (Longspoon Press, 1983); *The Alternate Guide* (Red Deer College Press, 1989); *These Lawns* (Red Deer College Press, 1990); *Crawlspace: New and Selected Poems* (House of Anansi, 1994); *Dog Sleeps: Irritated Texts* (NeWest Press, 1995); *Flat Side* (Red Deer College Press, 1998).

KEN RIVARD

Kiss Me Down to Size (Thistledown Press, 1983); *Losing His Thirst* (Pierian Press, 1985); *Frankie's Desires* (Quarry Press, 1987); *If She Could Take All These Men* (Beach Holme Publishers, 1995).

JAY RUZESKY

What Was Left of James Dean (Press On, 1992); *Am I Glad to See You* (Thistledown Press, 1992); *Painting the Yellow House Blue* (House of Anansi Press, 1994); *Blue Himalayan Poppies* (Reference West Press, 1995).

BARBARA SAPERGIA

Dirt Hills Mirage (Thistledown Press, 1980).

STEPHEN SCRIVER

Between the Lines (Thistledown Press, 1977); *All Star Poet!* (Coteau Books, 1981); *Under the Wings* (Coteau Books, 1992).

GREG SIMISON

Disturbances (Thistledown Press, 1981); *The Possibilities of Chinese Trout* (Okanagan College Press, 1986); *What the Wound Remembers* (Borealis Press, 1993).

GLEN SORESTAD

Wind Songs (Thistledown Press, 1975); *Prairie Pub Poems* (Thistledown, 1976); *Pear Seeds in My Mouth* (Sesame Press, 1977); *Ancestral Dances* (Thistledown Press, 1979); *Jan Lake Poems* (Harbour Publishing, 1984) *Hold the Rain in Your Hands* (Coteau Books, 1985); *Stalking Place* (with Peter Christensen and Jim Harris) (Hawk Press, 1988); *Air Canada Owls* (Nightwood Editions, 1990); *West Into Night* (Thistledown Press, 1991); *Jan Lake Sharing* (with Jim Harris) (1993); *Birchbark Meditations* (Writers on the Plains, New Mexico, 1996); *Icons of Flesh* (Ekstasis Editions, 1998).

RICHARD STEVENSON

Driving Offensively (Sono Nis Press, 1985); *Suiting Up* (Third Eye Press, 1986); *Horizontal Hotel: A Nigerian Odyssey* (Tsar Publications, 1989); *Whatever it is Plants Dream* (Goose Lane Editions, 1990); *Learning to Breathe* (Cacanadadada Press, 1992); *From the Mouths of Angels* (Ekstasis Editions, 1993); *Flying Coffins* (Ekstasis Editions, 1994); *Why Were All the Werewolves Men?* (Thistledown Press, 1994); *Wiser Pills* (HMS Books-on-disk, 1995); *A Murder of Crows: New and Selected Poems* (Black Moss Press, 1998).

GERTRUDE STORY

The Book of Thirteen (Thistledown Press, 1981).

DON SUMMERHAYES

Winter Apples (The Studio Press, 1982); *Heavy Horse Judging* (Thistledown Press, 1987); *Watermelon* (DEOR Editions, 1992); *Remembering Sleep* (DEOR Editions, 1993).

EVA TIHANYI

A Sequence of the Blood (Aya Press, 1983); *Prophecies Near the Speed of Light* (Thistledown Press, 1984); *Saved by the Telling* (Thistledown Press, 1995).

TOM WAYMAN

Waiting for Wayman (McClelland & Stewart, 1973); *For and Against the Moon* (Macmillan of Canada, 1974); *Money and Rain* (Macmillan of Canada, 1975); *Free Time* (Macmillan of Canada, 1977); *A Planet Mostly Sea* (Turnstone Press, 1979); *Living on the Ground* (McClelland & Stewart,

1980); *Introducing Tom Wayman: Selected Poems 1973-80* (Ontario Review Press, 1980); *The Nobel Prize Acceptance Speech* (Thistledown Press, 1981); *Counting the Hours* (McClelland & Stewart, 1983); *The Face of Jack Munro* (Harbour Publishing, 1986); *In a Small House on the Outskirts of Heaven* (Harbour Publishing, 1989); *Did I Miss Anything?: Selected Poems 1973-1993* (Harbour Publishing, 1993); *The Astonishing Weight of the Dead* (Polestar Press, 1994); *I'll Be Right Back: New & Selected Poems 1980-1996* (Ontario Review Press, 1997).

LYLE WEIS

The Mill Under His Skin (Thistledown Press, 1992).

GEORGE WHIPPLE

Life Cycle (Hownslow Press, 1984); *Passing Through Eden* (Thistledown Press, 1991); *Hats Off to the Sun* (Ekstasis Editions, 1996).

ANDREW WREGGITT

Riding to Nicola County (Harbour Publishing, 1981); *Man at Stellaco River* (Thistledown Press, 1984); *Southeasterly* (Thistledown Press, 1987); *Making Movies* (Thistledown Press, 1989); *Zhivago's Fire* (Thistledown Press, 1997).

THE EDITORS

ALLAN FORRIE teaches English at Evan Hardy Collegiate in Saskatoon. For more than two decades he has been an editor and book designer for Thistledown Press. He co-edited the anthologies *Dancing Visions* (Thistledown Press, 1985) and *The Last Map is the Heart* (Thistledown Press, 1989).

PATRICK O"ROURKE has been a career English teacher for thirty years, the past twenty-three years in the employ of the Saskatoon Board of Education. He is editor-in-chief of Thistledown Press. He co-edited the anthologies *Dancing Visions* (Thistledown Press, 1985) and *The Last Map is the Heart* (Thistledown Press, 1989).

GLEN SORESTAD is a Saskatoon writer and editor. He has published several books of poetry, most recently *West Into Night* and *Icons of Flesh*. As an anthologist he has co-edited numerous anthologies, among them *The Last Map is the Heart* (Thistledown Press, 1989).

PRINTED AND BOUND
IN BOUCHERVILLE, QUÉBEC, CANADA
BY MARC VEILLEUX IMPRIMEUR INC.
IN AUGUST, 1998